"What a marvelously conceived and well-executed project! Follow master teacher Jonathan Kline as he introduces the reader to the too often neglected book of Proverbs, demonstrates the value of its pithy sayings and aphorisms, and teaches Hebrew grammar and vocabulary all in a single stroke. The organization of the book allows all this to unfold in the most pedagogically beneficial way: Kline begins with the verses constructed from the most basic and common words, and only toward book's end does one encounter those proverbs that include rare lexical items. Students and scholars at all stages of learning will profit from this invaluable companion to the book of Proverbs."

**—Gary A. Rendsburg, Blanche and Irving Laurie**
**Professor of Jewish History, Rutgers University**

"Acquiring wisdom requires tedious grappling with proverbs, sayings, and riddles (Proverbs 1:6), many of them terse and obscure—some virtually impenetrable. Having navigated the path ahead of us, Kline is our able tutor on a difficult but rewarding journey. Every bit as clever as the sayings themselves, this book is part Hebrew grammar, part devotional, part poetry, and part introduction to wisdom literature. This little book achieves a style of translation that the eminent Hebrew translator Robert Alter believes is sadly lacking in our modern English Bibles."

**—Ryan P. O'Dowd, author of *Proverbs***
**(The Story of God Bible Commentary) and co-author of**
***Old Testament Wisdom Literature: A Theological Introduction***

"Jonathan Kline breathes new life into the book of Proverbs through this practical, smart guide. Both a devotional and a language tool, *A Proverb a Day in Biblical Hebrew* gently leads its users through difficult syntax and at times perplexing content, giving us more than enough each day to pronounce in Hebrew, to read, and to think about throughout the day. Students, seminarians, and pastors who have taken even a year or two of Hebrew will be able to track with the language of Proverbs through Kline's expert guidance. I highly recommend this book both as a language-learning tool and as a year-long devotional journey through the wisdom of Proverbs."

**—Brian R. Doak**
**Associate Professor of Biblical Studies**
**George Fox University**

"Thank you, Jonathan Kline, for this helpful and carefully presented guide to reading Proverbs in Hebrew one day at a time. I enthusiastically recommend this book to all who want to keep up and improve their Hebrew skills. Not only will the reader's language ability grow, but so will their knowledge of the book of Proverbs. If you want to grow in wisdom, read Proverbs; and if you want to grow in your understanding of Proverbs, read *A Proverb a Day in Biblical Hebrew*."

**—Tremper Longman III, Distinguished Scholar and Professor Emeritus of Biblical Studies, Westmont College**

"This book has so many good qualities to commend it: it is informed, it will encourage flagging Hebrew readers, it is brief enough to be doable for most of us—and even more, it helps us to tap daily into the glories of the wisdom culture that comes to expression in these proverbs. Ours is a world swamped by everything new, while Proverbs takes us into a world where the old is ever renewable. Daily ponderings of wisdom make for a wise person."

**—Scot McKnight, Professor of New Testament, Northern Seminary**

"Kline understands that proverbs are meant for daily use, to be read regularly and continually pondered. *A Proverb a Day in Biblical Hebrew* facilitates that practice and reminds readers of the challenge, the intriguing nature, and the fun of these Hebrew sayings."

**—Arthur J. Keefer, Chaplain and Teacher of Theology Eton College, United Kingdom**

"*A Proverb a Day in Biblical Hebrew* encourages readers to digest select biblical proverbs slowly in order to contemplate their often subtle and multilayered meanings. . . . This handy workbook forces readers to realize that Hebrew texts cannot be read like Twitter accounts, but must be mined carefully for their intellectual depths. It is ideal for beginning students or informed lay readers who want to improve their knowledge of Hebrew and their appreciation for the sophisticated wisdom of the Israelites."

**—Scott B. Noegel Professor of Biblical and Ancient Near Eastern Studies University of Washington**

**A Proverb a Day in Biblical Hebrew**

© 2019 by Hendrickson Publishers Marketing, LLC
P. O. Box 3473
Peabody, Massachusetts 01961-3473
www.hendrickson.com

ISBN 978-1-68307-243-0

*Printed in the United States of America*

*First Printing — August 2019*

Vector design by Venimo via Getty Images.
Cover and wrap design by Karol Bailey.

### Library of Congress Cataloging-in-Publication Data

Names: Kline, Jonathan G., author.
Title: A proverb a day in biblical Hebrew / compiled and edited by
    Jonathan G. Kline.
Description: Peabody, Massachusetts : Hendrickson Publishers Marketing,
    LLC, [2019] | Includes bibliographical references and indexes.
Identifiers: LCCN 2019011158 | ISBN 9781683072430 (alk. paper)
Subjects: LCSH: Hebrew language--Self-instruction. | Bible.
    Proverbs--Language, style.
Classification: LCC PJ4567.5 .K44 2019 | DDC 223/.7044--dc23
    LC record available at https://lccn.loc.gov/2019011158

# A PROVERB A DAY IN BIBLICAL HEBREW

Compiled and edited by Jonathan G. Kline

HENDRICKSON PUBLISHERS

# Contents

# Preface

*A Proverb a Day in Biblical Hebrew* has been designed to help you mull over, chew on, and slowly digest one verse from the book of Proverbs on a regular basis (ideally each day, as the book's title suggests).[1] Like the delicious morsels of a gourmet meal (to continue the alimentary analogy, and to play on the image found in 18:8 and 26:22), the proverbs that have been bequeathed to us from ancient Israel are best appreciated and internalized by savoring them slowly and in small quantities. This is true for at least two reasons. First, the primary purpose of these sayings is to shape the reader's or listener's thinking, character, and actions, and an excellent way to facilitate such personal transformation is to reflect on— and, as need be, puzzle over—one of the proverbs in a meditative spirit throughout the course of an entire day (or longer). Second, it is helpful to read the proverbs in a slow and focused manner simply because they can be difficult to understand, on account of the fact that—certainly in the original, and even sometimes in translation—they are terse and at times cryptic, ambiguous, or polysemous in nature.

Indeed, there are a number of specific reasons why the biblical proverbs can be hard to comprehend, even for those who are able to read other poetic portions of the Hebrew Bible without too much difficulty. While some of the proverbs speak to us directly on account of their universality (e.g., 12:18, "There's one who speaks rashly, like sword thrusts" [Day 295]), others are more obscure given the cultural and temporal

---

1. Each page is labeled with a day number (from 1 to 365), a date (from January 1 to December 31), and a week number (from Week 1 to Week 52). The book is thus designed so that you can work through it in a calendar year (whether starting on January 1 or any other date), though of course you need not use it according to this scheme.

gulf that separates us from the ancient Israelites.[2] Occasionally we come across idioms in these adages whose meanings are not intuitive to us: for example, "hand to hand" (Prov 11:21 [Day 240]; 16:5 [Day 165]) or "to dig evil" (Prov 16:27 [Day 242]). At other times we encounter difficulties of syntax: for example, when a nominal predicate (generally the more narrow category) precedes a nominal subject (typically the broader category), which is the opposite of standard English order (see, e.g., 15:27 [Day 354]). In some instances the basic meanings of the individual words in a proverb are clear enough, but how the words work together to create a meaningful utterance may not be immediately obvious—as, for example, in Prov 20:6a (רָב־אָדָם יִקְרָא אִישׁ חַסְדּוֹ), found on Day 51. And on still other occasions, a proverb's vocabulary and syntax may both be straightforward, but its meaning as a whole may be ambiguous (a well-known example being Prov 22:6 [Day 210]).

As if all this were not enough, a final factor that can make it difficult to understand these ancient adages of the sages is that some, perhaps many, of them (especially the one-verse sayings in chapters 10–29) appear to be largely or even completely unconnected to the others that surround them in their present, canonical arrangement. Hence, unlike in most parts of the Bible, in Proverbs 10–29 context usually does not offer very much help for understanding what vocabulary, imagery, or subject matter to expect in a given verse. That said, scholars do acknowledge the presence of small clusters of sayings in this corpus that are related to each other by sound, vocabulary, or meaning; and occasionally the interplay between two juxtaposed proverbs is in fact essential for grasping their nature.[3]

---

2. See, for example, the verses that talk about "standing surety" or making pledges—11:15 (Day 279), 17:18 (Day 198), and 20:16 (Day 333)—or 20:26 (Day 219), which uses the image of the king rolling a wheel over evildoers, as if they were grain undergoing threshing.

3. Most famously, perhaps, 26:4–5—the proverbs about answering a fool according to his folly—reflect the fact that the same action can be wise in some situations but unwise in others. On proverb clusters, see especially Knut M. Heim, *Like Grapes of Gold Set in Silver: An Interpretation of Proverbial Clusters in Proverbs 10:1–22:16* (BZAW 273; Berlin: de Gruyter, 2001); for a brief over-

Nevertheless, most commentators have not been able to discern a large or detailed structure in these chapters.[4]

When all of the aforementioned obstacles are compounded by the normal challenges that most contemporary students of ancient Hebrew encounter when they try to read any portion of the biblical text in its original language, many give up the prospect of ever reading the biblical proverbs in Hebrew. *A Proverb a Day in Biblical Hebrew* is designed to help you overcome these hurdles by empowering you to read this part of the biblical corpus with confidence and understanding. It does so by providing one verse on each page and everything you need to work through the verse on your own: context-specific glosses for each of the words, parsings for all verb forms (including participles), and a full translation of the verse.

## The Verses

This book presents all but ten of the 375 verses that comprise "The Proverbs of Solomon" (10:1), the section that spans 10:1 to 22:16, which is the largest generally recognized collection of sayings found in the book. *A Proverb a Day in Biblical Hebrew* therefore contains about 40 percent of the text of the book of Proverbs—that is, 365 of the book's 915 verses. Thus, by the time you have worked through the present volume, you should feel well equipped to read the rest of the book of Proverbs in Hebrew with confidence.

As is well known, some of the verses in Proverbs are identical, or (more often) nearly so, to other verses in the book. In order to whittle down the 375 verses in 10:1–22:16 to fit the present book's 365-day scheme, I have taken advantage of the existence of (nearly) verbatim sayings by

---

view, see Michael V. Fox, *Proverbs 10–31: A New Translation with Introduction and Commentary* (Anchor Yale Bible 18B; New Haven: Yale University Press, 2009), 477–83. A helpful recent discussion on this topic, specifically as it relates to the proverbs that speak about pain, is Ryan P. O'Dowd, "Pain and Danger: Unpleasant Sayings and the Structure of Proverbs," *Catholic Biblical Quarterly* 80 (2018): 631–34.

4. O'Dowd, "Pain and Danger," 631.

omitting from this book the ten verses in this corpus that are identical to (in one case) or most nearly identical to (in the other nine cases) other verses in the corpus.[5]

The verses in this book are presented not in canonical order but rather according to the number of times the words they contain appear in Prov 10:1–22:16. That is to say, the verses with the highest number of frequently occurring words are located at the beginning, and the verses with the highest number of infrequently occurring words are located at the end.[6] The result of this organizational scheme is that you will continue to encounter the same words over and over as you make your way through the book, with the more frequently occurring ones fronted in the early pages to help you master the vocabulary found in Prov 10:1–22:16 efficiently.[7] That said, the difficulty of the morphology and syntax

5. Specifically, I have omitted 11:4 (~ 10:2), 11:7 (~ 10:28), 14:27 (~ 13:14), 15:20 (~ 10:1), 15:22 (~ 11:14), 16:25 (= 14:12), 17:22 (~ 15:13), 19:9 (~ 19:5), 20:23 (~ 11:1), and 21:2 (~ 16:2). For a full list of similar verses in the book of Proverbs, see Daniel C. Snell, *Twice-Told Proverbs and the Composition of the Book of Proverbs* (Winona Lake, IN: Eisenbrauns, 1993), 34–59; see also, more recently, Knut M. Heim, *Poetic Imagination in Proverbs: Variant Repetitions and the Nature of Poetry* (Winona Lake, IN: Eisenbrauns, 2013).

6. Specifically, all of the words found on Days 1–3 occur in Prov 10:1–22:16 seven times or more; therefore, you will encounter each of these words repeatedly as you continue through the book. All of the words appearing on Days 4–8 occur in Prov 10:1–22:16 six times or more; the words on Days 9–14, five times or more; the words on Days 15–26, four times or more; the words on Days 27–65, three times or more; and the words on Days 66–151, twice or more. Beginning with Day 152, each verse contains at least one word that occurs only once in Prov 10:1–22:16 (though the other words found on Days 152 through 365 may occur any number of times in the corpus). Nevertheless, these verses too (i.e., the ones comprising roughly the latter three-fifths of the book) are ordered according to how often you will continue to encounter the words they contain (the words on Day 152 having the largest combined total number of occurrences in Prov 10:1–22:16 and the words on Day 365 having the smallest combined total number of occurrences).

7. For those interested in exactly how many times each Hebrew word found in this book occurs in Prov 10:1–22:16, I have included a Frequency Index of Hebrew Words at the back of the book (note that this index groups homonyms together).

of the verses in this book does not proceed from easiest to hardest (indeed, such an organizational scheme would be difficult, if not impossible, to create). Thus, you will notice that, with respect to morphology and syntax, the verses will vary in difficulty as you make your way through the book. From a pedagogical standpoint, however, such variation can in fact be considered an advantage.

## The Glosses

When translating aphoristic poetry, there is often more than one legitimate or helpful way to render a given word. Therefore, for many of the Hebrew words in this book, I have provided more than one gloss (using a slash to separate alternatives, or double slashes when a single slash would be ambiguous), in order to give you a sense of the possible meanings or nuances that I believe may be in view in the verse in question, leaving you to ponder and judge their relative value for the context. I have erred on the side of inclusivity in this regard, though to reiterate, I have taken care to include only glosses that I consider to be at least potentially appropriate to the context (even if some may be more relevant than others).[8]

I have also erred on the side of literalness in my glosses, in order to help you engage as closely as possible with the Hebrew text and in order to highlight grammatical features that, being odd or unexpected from an English-speaker's point of view, are sometimes smoothed over or obscured in standard translations. Examples of this include my use of (odd-sounding) English plurals to gloss words that are plural in Hebrew but that English translations tend to render as singulars (e.g., "envoy of faithfuless*es*/honest*ies*" in Prov 13:17 [Day 231]), and my use of past-tense glosses for *wayyiqtol* verbs (of which there are only seven in

---

8. By including a number of glosses for many words in this book, I do not mean to encourage the so-called "illegitimate totality transfer" error, whereby one concludes that all possible meanings of a given word are, or at least might be, relevant for a specific context. Instead, I have provided multiple glosses in order to allow *you* to do the necessary and rewarding work of thinking through which one (or ones) you think best fits the context.

the present book) even when they are found in what appear to be apho-ristic statements (e.g., "***then*** (he) ***came***" for וַיָּבֹא in Prov 11:8 [Day 86]).

For many of the words that occur in this book (especially the more frequently occurring ones), I have provided a relatively fixed set of glosses, typically in a consistent order (e.g., "prudent/shrewd/clever" for עָרוּם), so that you can do the work of determining which gloss you think is best for each context. Nevertheless, for words of this kind I have varied the glosses, or their order, whenever I felt the context called for this.

On rare occasions, I have included a gloss that I think does not ac-tually reflect how a word should be translated or understood (at least in a primary sense) in context but that I nevertheless think might be in the background, for example, as a play on words. I have always set off such glosses in square brackets.[9]

I created the initial draft of the glosses on my own, occasionally consulting a standard lexicon or published translations, and sometimes surveying most or all of the instances of a word in the Bible in order to get a good sense of its semantic range. I then refined the glosses by consulting in detail several standard Hebrew lexicons,[10] various

---

9. See, for example, Prov 10:4 (Day 132), where I have included the admit-tedly odd gloss "[golds]" not because I think this is actually the meaning of חָרוּצִים in this verse, but rather (since חָרוּץ can mean "gold") because I wish to suggest that חָרוּצִים here may *possibly* (though it may not) be punning on the next word, תַּעֲשִׁיר "(it) becomes/makes *rich*." Likewise, in Prov 11:28 (Day 265), "One who trusts in his wealth—he will fall," the word בּוֹטֵחַ clearly means "one who trusts." However, given that there is another root בטח that means "fall," and in light of the fact that this poetic line ends with the verb יִפֹּל "he will fall," my inclusion of the bracketed gloss "[falls]" for בּוֹטֵחַ is intended to indicate that, although I do not think this word should be translated "falls" in context, I wonder whether the sage who wrote this proverb might have intended the word as a pun on יִפֹּל (i.e., "One who falls by his wealth—he will (indeed) fall!").

10. Especially David J. A. Clines, ed., *The Concise Dictionary of Classical Hebrew* (Sheffield: Sheffield Phoenix Press, 2009); Ludwig Koehler, Walter Baumgartner, and Johann J. Stamm, *The Hebrew and Aramaic Lexicon of the Old Testament: Study Edition*, trans. and ed. under the supervision of M. E. J. Richard-

translations,[11] and, especially for a handful of difficult verses, Michael Fox's excellent commentary.[12]

Despite the fact that I have consulted a number of sources in order to generate my glosses and have tried to present glosses that fit in each context, I have not undertaken in-depth research on most of the verses or words presented in this book. The book is not a technical commentary; instead, it is a language-learning and reading aid whose main goal is to help students, clergy, teachers, and scholars who have not yet read much of the book of Proverbs in Hebrew begin to explore how these sayings work in Hebrew and to think more critically about what they mean than is possible to do simply by reading them in translation. This volume provides you with the basic tools you need to wrestle intelligently with these sayings, but I encourage you to also consult published translations of and commentaries on these texts.

## Grammatical Constructions

I have done my best in this book to be as consistent as possible in how I have glossed specific grammatical constructions (e.g., prepositions followed by infinitives construct; participles), but the book naturally presents some variation in this regard, based on the demands of each verse's context and what I thought would be helpful from a pedagogical perspective. I do not have the space here to explain most of the choices I have made in glossing the various kinds of grammatical constructions encountered in these texts, and in any case the majority of my choices should become obvious as you work your way through the book. Nevertheless, I would like to make a few comments here on some of the specifics of my glossing method.

---

son (Leiden: Brill, 2001); William L. Holladay, ed., *A Concise Hebrew and Aramaic Lexicon of the Old Testament* (Grand Rapids: Eerdmans, 1971); Francis Brown, S. R. Driver, and Charles A. Briggs, *A Hebrew and English Lexicon of the Old Testament* (Boston: Houghton Mifflin, 1906; repr., Peabody, MA: Hendrickson, 1996).

11. Especially the NJPS, NRSV, NASB, ESV, NIV, and MLB.

12. See note 3 above.

First, I have put parentheses around any grammatical information in the glosses—for example, subject pronouns in glosses for verbal forms—that is an inherent part of a particular Hebrew form but that is inapplicable for translation in context. For example, in Prov 17:2 (Day 130), the pronoun "he" is in parentheses in "(he) will rule" because the clause has an explicit subject, עֶבֶד "servant/slave." By contrast, in Prov 16:31 (Day 126), the subject of the verb תִּמָּצֵא in the b-line—namely, שֵׂיבָה "old age/gray hair"—is located in the a-line (thus, in a different clause); hence the gloss "it is found" for תִּמָּצֵא, with no parentheses around "it."

Because participles are simultaneously nominal and verbal in character, I had to be thoughtful about how to gloss them. I decided to err on the side of consistency here: that is to say, regardless of their syntax in a particular context (indeed, in order to *prompt* you to think about their syntax), I have glossed participles as "one who . . ." (or, for the occasional participle that refers to an impersonal or non-count entity, "one that . . ." or "that which . . . ," respectively). In keeping with what I said above regarding parentheses, I have put parentheses around "one" or "one who" if these words are not relevant for English translation. However, when a subject and a predicate are both participles, I have used "one who" (without parentheses) for both glosses, in order to leave it up to you to decide which participle is the subject and which is the predicate, something that is not always clear at first and that sometimes is genuinely ambiguous.

Although I have normally placed each Hebrew word on its own line, I have made an exception to this practice in a few kinds of cases, the most common of which is that I have placed the two (or three) words of a construct chain on a single line, given their close syntactic relationship to one another. In accord with this principle, when a participle is a *nomen rectum* (and therefore its nominal character is more pronounced), I have placed it on the same line as the word that is (or words that are) in construct to it. However, when a participle is a *nomen regens* (and therefore its verbal character is more pronounced), I have put the *nomen rectum* of the construct chain on a separate line (since, at least from an English perspective, the participle in this case effectively functions as a finite verb and the *nomen rectum* as its direct object).[13]

When translating the proverbs, English-speakers often need to supply an indefinite or definite article to denote a general category (e.g., "*a* wise man" rather than simply "wise man"; or "*the* righteous," i.e., "righteous people"). Hebrew has no indefinite article, of course, and I have therefore omitted "a" from my glosses, so that you can decide when you think adding it in English is appropriate.[14] The Hebrew (definite) article rarely appears in Prov 10:1–22:16. In order to reflect this fact and to draw your attention to the occasions when it does appear,[15] I have typically glossed substantive adjectives referring to human beings with a translation of the adjective in question followed by "person" (when the adjective is singular) or "people" (when the adjective is plural), without inserting "the" (or "a") as part of the gloss (e.g., עָצֵל "lazy person"; רְשָׁעִים "wicked people").

For the sake of simplicity, I have typically glossed Imperfect and Perfect verbs with the English present tense when they occur in what in my judgment is a statement of a general or universal principle.[16] I have always glossed *wayyiqtol* verbs with the word "then" (or "but," in one case) plus a past-tense verb, in order to bring your attention to these forms, which are rare in the proverbs and which indeed are somewhat surprising

---

13. An exception is that when a participle that is a *nomen regens* is passive, and hence functioning adjectivally, I have kept the *nomen rectum* on the same line as the participle. See, e.g., Prov 22:14 (Day 223).

14. I have omitted "a" even before my glosses for the second or third noun in a construct chain, in which case the omission of the article sounds particularly odd (e.g., "fruit of mouth of man"). This is one aspect of my having erred on the side of literalness in my glosses.

15. Interestingly, in such cases it is sometimes inappropriate to translate with English "the": e.g., כַּחֹמֶץ לַשִּׁנַּיִם "like vinegar to the teeth" (lit., "like *the* vinegar to the teeth") in Prov 10:26 (Day 346).

16. When employing a future-tense English gloss seemed more appropriate to the context, however, I have done so.

to find in sayings that appear to be aphoristic in nature.[17] Finally, I have glossed *weqatal* verbs with either "and . . ." or "then . . .".

## The Parsings

I have provided parsing for all verbs, including participles. Each parsing is presented on its own line, where it is indented and set in a different font than the one used for the glosses.[18]

Some Hebrew words can be analyzed in more than one way. For example, some participles that typically have a substantival or adjectival function in the Bible are commonly parsed as nouns or adjectives: e.g., יוֹעֵץ "counselor" (noun or Qal Ptcp ms יעץ), אוֹיֵב "enemy" (noun or Qal Ptcp ms איב), שָׂמֵחַ "happy" (adj or Qal Ptcp ms שמח). In most such cases, I have chosen one parsing rather than indicating both of the possibilities (notwithstanding the fact that both may be equally legitimate). For a handful of words whose parsing is more complex or interesting, however, I have provided more than one option. One of the more striking examples of this in the book is probably the word יָפִיחַ, which, depending on the context, can be analyzed either as a noun meaning "witness" or as a verb (Hiph Impf 3ms of פוח) meaning "he breathes out." Likewise, when a verb can plausibly be parsed in more than one way in context, I have provided both parsings (or in one case, Prov 18:24 [Day 303], three).

---

17. In this way, I am attempting to emphasize the "micro-narrative" aspect of verses containing *wayyiqtols*. (I occasionally also gloss Perfects with past-tense English verbs for the same reason; see, e.g., Prov 22:3 [Day 149].) For a brief discussion of the concept of "micro-narratives" in the book of Proverbs—though not only for verses containing *wayyiqtol* forms—see O'Dowd, "Pain and Danger," 628–29.

18. I created the parsings found in this book on my own and then occasionally checked them against Clines, *Concise Dictionary of Classical Hebrew*; Holladay, *Concise Hebrew and Aramaic Lexicon of the Old Testament*; and/or Fox, *Proverbs 10–31*.

The following abbreviations appear among the parsings found in this book:[19]

| 1    | first-person  | Impv | Imperative  |
|------|---------------|------|-------------|
| 2    | second-person | Inf  | Infinitive  |
| 3    | third-person  | Juss | Jussive     |
| Abs  | Absolute      | m    | masculine   |
| c    | common        | Niph | Niphal      |
| Coh  | Cohortative   | p    | plural      |
| conj | conjunction   | Pass | Passive     |
| Cst  | Construct     | Pf   | Perfect     |
| f    | feminine      | prep | preposition |
| Hiph | Hiphil        | Ptcp | Participle  |
| Hith | Hithpael      | s    | singular    |
| Hoph | Hophal        | sx   | suffix      |
| Impf | Imperfect     |      |             |

## The Hebrew Text

The Hebrew text used in *A Proverb a Day in Biblical Hebrew* has been taken from the Michigan-Claremont-Westminster Electronic Hebrew Bible, a popular electronic version that is based on the BHS and that has been revised by its creators on the basis of comparison with the Leningrad Codex. This electronic text is in the public domain and has been made available courtesy of the J. Alan Groves Center for Advanced Biblical Research. In a few cases, I have corrected the reading of this text against that of Aron Dotan's *Biblia Hebraica Leningradensia* (Peabody, MA: Hendrickson, 2001) when I judged the latter to be superior (for example, I changed the Westminster text's reading מֵרֵעֵהוּ in Prov 19:4

---

19. Note that although I have abbreviated the names of four of the major *binyanim* (Niph, Hiph, Hoph, Hith), I have spelled out the shorter stem names (Qal, Piel, and Pual) as well as—for the sake of clarity and because they occur only infrequently in the book—the names of uncommon stems (Polel, Pilpel, Hithpoel, Hithpolel).

[Day 137] to Dotan's reading, מֵרֵעֵהוּ, which is also the reading found in the Aleppo Codex).

For simplicity's sake, and because this book is a language-learning and reading tool rather than a work of technical scholarship, whenever there is a Ketiv-Qere I have included only the Qere form in the main text.[20] However, I have presented all Ketiv forms (of which there are 26 in the book) parenthetically, which is to say, in the same manner in which parsings are marked (on their own line, indented, and in a different font from that of the main text).

## Text-Critical Issues

Some of the proverbs found in 10:1–22:16 contain grammatical or text-critical difficulties. Since my goal in creating this book has primarily been to help you engage closely with the Masoretic Text as it stands (specifically as it is attested in the Leningrad Codex), I have made no attempt to solve these kinds of difficulties, and the format of this book has typically not allowed me to draw your attention to them explicitly. I take this opportunity, therefore, to make a few general remarks on this subject.

Occasionally a verse in this book seems to be corrupt or incomprehensible as it stands. The most obvious case of this is Prov 19:7 (Day 104), whose a-line is the length of most of the proverbs' a- and b-lines combined and the meaning of whose b-line (מְרַדֵּף אֲמָרִים לֹו־הֵמָּה) is quite obscure. Fox omits this b-line from his translation altogether, calling it "an unintelligible fragment" and "a meaningless group of four words … [that] looks like the mangled fragment of a lost couplet."[21] For this verse, I have provided a literal (and thus ungrammatical) translation in order to draw your attention to the presence of this difficulty.

---

20. This does not imply, however, that I always believe the Qere provides the best or most reasonable reading. Indeed, my translations (on which see further below), in distinction to my glosses, occasionally follow the Ketiv: see, for example, Prov 12:14 (Day 69), where my translation "and the deed of a person's hands *will rebound* to him" follows the Ketiv (ישוב) rather than the Qere (יָשִׁיב).

21. Fox, *Proverbs 10–31*, 650–51.

In other cases, the basic meaning of a verse seems clear, but a grammatical difficulty is nevertheless present.[22] For all such cases that involve verbs, I have placed the siglum "(!)" in the verb's parsing line in order to indicate the oddity or corruption (e.g., "3ms(!)" when "3mp" would be the parsing of the expected form).[23] Since non-verbs are not parsed in this book, for verses that contain a grammatical difficulty involving a non-verb I have not marked the difficulty with "(!)" (since doing so in the gloss section could erroneously imply that it is the gloss itself that is problematic);[24] in such cases, therefore, I have simply left it up to you to notice the difficulty yourself.[25]

## The English Translations

As has been reiterated throughout this preface, the goal of this book is to empower you to work through the biblical proverbs on your own. It is often interesting and helpful while doing so to compare your understanding of a verse to that of other people, however, especially for verses whose syntax or vocabulary is difficult or may involve polysemy; indeed,

---

22. For example, the number (or gender) of a predicate may not agree with that of the subject (e.g., וְאֹהֲבֶיהָ יֹאכַל in Prov 18:21 [Day 27]), or the form of a word may be odd or corrupt (e.g., תִּשְׁמוּרֵם in Prov 14:3 [Day 196]).

23. Thus, for example, I have parsed תִּשְׁמוּרֵם in Prov 14:3 as a Qal Impf "3fs(!)" of שׁמר with 3mp suffix, even though the word seems to be a corruption of תִּשְׁמְרוּם, which is a Qal Impf 3fp of שׁמר with 3mp suffix (see Fox, *Proverbs 10–31*, 573, on this parsing of the base form, though note that he states that the suffix is "3 masc. sg.").

24. I have made one exception to this practice, however, by inserting "(!)" amid the glosses for the last word in Prov 11:25 (Day 287), namely, יוֹרֶא, a verbal form that would seem to be from the root ירה "to teach" but that the context seems to demand should actually be understood as a form of רוה "to water" (hence my gloss "will teach (!)").

25. Typically such difficulties are rather obvious, as in Prov 12:10 (Day 175), where the adjective אַכְזְרִי is singular even though it modifies the plural noun רַחֲמֵי "compassions," and as in Prov 16:33 (Day 216), where the definite direct *object* marker, אֶת־, precedes the *subject*, הַגּוֹרָל.

in such cases, consulting the translations of others can be essential for thinking through what may be going on in the verse. For this reason, after you work through each verse in this book on your own, I encourage you, as stated earlier, to look at as many published translations of and commentaries on the book of Proverbs as may be helpful.

In addition, and for your convenience, I have created my own translation of each verse in this book. Since I do not wish to bias or influence your initial reading of the text by means of my own translations, however, I have placed each translation not at the bottom of the page for each day's Hebrew verse, but rather two pages thereafter, so that you will always need to consciously decide to turn the page if you wish to see my translation.[26]

Because for each day's Hebrew verse I have glossed every word on the page for the day (including providing multiple glosses for many words, as mentioned above), the primary purpose of my translations is *not* to help you grasp the basic meanings of the words in the verse but *rather* to help you understand the verse's *syntax* and *overall meaning*—in other words, to help you check if you are "putting all the pieces together" in a way that makes sense. For this reason, as far as word choice is concerned, I have allowed myself to be somewhat creative in my translations. Largely this has involved my drawing deeply from the rich reservoir of English vocabulary and alternating between short words of Anglo-Saxon origin and polysyllabic Latinate vocables. The result is a set of translations that I hope will strike you as fresh, memorable, and—by dint of their novelty—defamiliarizing, thought-provoking, and even fun.

To give you a sense for the style I have used, here are a few randomly selected examples of my translations: "The commencement of contention is a crack in the dike; so before a fight flares up, stop" (17:14 [Day 329]); "The lot puts an end to litigiousness, and it splits up strong men" (18:18 [Day 361]); and "Every shrewd man acts with skill, but a numbskull disseminates stupidity" (13:16 [Day 197]). As these examples illustrate, in addition to using the technique of combining terse and ornate

---

26. E.g., my translation for Prov 12:15, the Hebrew verse found on Day 6, is located at the bottom of the Day 8 page; and so on.

vocabulary, I frequently employ soundplay and rhythm for poetic effect.[27] In a few instances I have taken more than a little poetic license in this regard: e.g., Prov 17:12 (Day 233), "Better to meet a bereaved bear than a boor on a bender" (the b-stich here in Hebrew reads "but not a dolt in his folly," which is clear from the glosses I provide two pages earlier, hence my indulgence in a rather creative rendering here). For fun, I have occasionally employed other varieties of wordplay in my translations as well.[28] Finally, on rare occasions, I have used vocabulary that serves to transpose the biblical text into a modern conceptual framework, in order to give the proverb contemporary relevance; an example is 16:8 (Day 61), which I have translated "Better limited assets acquired honestly than an immense net worth amassed by mendacity."

As a counterbalance to my creativity, and to respect the proverbs' concision and the fact that some are ambiguous, I have attempted to err on the side of literalness and underinterpretation of the text, especially with

---

27. This is in part an homage to the biblical writers themselves, whose penchant for using soundplay as a productive compositional factor in fashioning their writings is well known. For brief overviews of this topic, see Scott B. Noegel, "Paronomasia," *Encyclopedia of Hebrew Language and Linguistics*, ed. Geoffrey Khan (Leiden: Brill, 2013), 3:24–29; Jonathan G. Kline, *Allusive Soundplay in the Hebrew Bible* (SBLAIL 28; Atlanta: SBL Press, 2016), esp. 6–17 (with relevant bibliography on p. 8 note 19). A thorough survey of scholarship on this subject can be found in Arthur Keefer, "Phonological Patterns in the Hebrew Bible: A Century of Studies in Sound," *Currents in Biblical Research* 15 (2016): 41–64. On the use of soundplay in Proverbs in particular, see Arthur Keefer, "Sound Patterns as Motivation for Rare Words in Proverbs 1–9," *Journal of Northwest Semitic Languages* 43 (2017): 35–49; Thomas P. McCreesh, *Biblical Sound and Sense: Poetic Sound Patterns in Proverbs 10–29* ( JSOTSup 128; Sheffield: Sheffield Academic, 1991).

28. Examples include my use of Janus parallelism, via the word "capital," in Prov 10:15 (Day 145), and my appreciative nod to the wordplay (specifically, polysemy) created by the use of the Hebrew word בַּר "clean/grain" in Prov 14:4 (Day 344) through the use of a pair of paronomastic English words, "barn" and "brawn," both of which contain this word's consonants, /b/ and /r/, and which thus play on its sound. ("Barn" is, of course, not a literal translation of אֵבוּס, which means "trough/manger," though the concepts are related by means of synecdoche.)

regard to rendering pronouns. An example of this is Prov 14:32 (Day 187), which I have translated "A devilish man is overthrown by his evil, and a righteous man takes refuge in his demise." To whom does "his" in the b-line refer—the righteous man or the devilish man? Some published translations (e.g., NJPS, ESV) retain this ambiguity, but others (e.g., NRSV, NIV) make the more theologically comfortable of the two possible interpretations explicit, sometimes by effectively emending the text.[29] For this verse, I have decided to reflect the ambiguity of the Hebrew in my translation in order to draw your attention to it and to prompt you to think through the possible interpretations and their implications. For other ambiguous verses, however, the act of translating has forced me to make an interpretive choice;[30] at the very least, my glosses (i.e., the ones found two pages prior to my translation) should make the ambiguities in such cases clear.[31]

In sum, I hope that my translations encourage you to heartily embrace the interesting and rewarding, if sometimes difficult, task of crafting your own renderings, a process that can help these sayings come to life for you in new ways and make them more meaningful for your own experience.

## Gendered and Gender-Neutral Language

In this book I have tried my best to provide glosses and translations that are faithful to the Hebrew text as well as clear and interesting in English, and

---

29. NRSV: "but the righteous find a refuge in their integrity"; NIV: "but even in death the righteous seek refuge in God." See also NASB: "But the righteous has a refuge when he dies" (in theory, though, this translation could be considered ambiguous).

30. See, for example, Prov 13:13 (Day 144), where scholars and translations disagree about how to render the verb חבל and where I have simply chosen one of the options for my translation.

31. In some cases of this sort, I have chosen a translation that reflects a minority or nonstandard interpretation, not necessarily because I believe it is always the best one, but in order to present you with a different point of view from that offered in most published translations. An example of this is found in my translation of Prov 22:6 (Day 210): "Give a youth over to his path; then, when he's old, he won't turn away from it."

that are also, as often as seemed possible and reasonable, gender-neutral. Nevertheless, since this book is primarily a language-learning tool, I have erred on the side of reflecting the gender-specific nature of the Hebrew in English whenever I thought this would help you understand the original text better. In addition, since the book of Proverbs was written primarily for the consumption of elite young men in a culture in which the majority of power was held by males,[32] I hope that when you encounter gender-specific English terms in both my glosses and my translations, this will prompt you—as it has me—to think more deeply about and wrestle with the assumptions and worldview espoused by the authors and original intended audience of this book.

A few specific comments on my use of gender-neutral language are worth making here. First, in my glosses, I have tried whenever possible to render generic words such as אִישׁ, בֵּן, and אָבוֹת both with a standard gender-specific term and with a gender-neutral equivalent (e.g., "man/person," "son/child," "fathers/parents"). In addition, I have glossed substantive masculine singular adjectives, such as צַדִּיק "righteous," in a gender-neutral fashion—that is, as "righteous *person*" rather than "righteous *man*." Likewise, and as noted earlier in this preface, I have rendered masculine (as well as feminine) singular participles as "*one* who . . ." (rather than "*he* who . . ." or "*she* who . . .").

In contrast to this, in my translation of any given verse I was naturally unable to provide both a gender-specific and a gender-neutral rendering of a single Hebrew word. For this reason, when translating words that in Hebrew are gender-specific I have alternated between gender-neutral terms such as "person" or "one" and gender-specific terms such as "man" or "he," depending on what I thought made the most sense in context and also for stylistic reasons (e.g., for the sake of rhythm or to create soundplay). In addition, because (again) this book's main purpose is to help you understand what the Hebrew text says, in my translations I have attempted as much as possible to retain singular and plural

---

32. One facet of this is the rarity with which women are even mentioned in Prov 10:1–22:16.

distinctions that are present in the Hebrew. This has meant that, unlike some published translations, I have chosen not to render singulars that are gender-specific (e.g., "man," "his") with gender-neutral plurals (e.g., "people," "their"), since—although this has the merit of communicating the meaning of the text in a gender-neutral fashion—it obscures the grammar of the Hebrew.

\* \* \* \* \*

I would like to express my deep gratitude to my friend and intrepid colleague Phil Frank, who expertly typeset this book and (as he also did for previous language tools of this kind that I have created) offered camaraderie and invaluable advice and constructive criticism that helped strengthen the volume. I am also grateful to my colleague Tirzah Frank for her incisive editorial eye and for her helpful criticisms, which improved the book in a number of respects, as well as to my colleague Amy Paulsen-Reed for suggesting various useful revisions.

I offer this book in friendship to you, the reader, and with the hope that as you work through the proverbs it contains you will grow in wisdom and humility and that you will develop a more profound love for truth and a more expansive compassion for others—especially the poor, the needy, and the oppressed, who are continually mentioned in these pages. May we all seek to deepen these essential character traits in ourselves and in each other, which are so vital for the flourishing of our families, our communities, and our world.

—Jonathan G. Kline, PhD

קֹנֶה־לֵּב אֹהֵב נַפְשׁוֹ

| | |
|---|---|
| קֹנֶה־ | *one who acquires/gets/gains/obtains* |
| | Qal Ptcp ms קנה |
| לֵּב | *heart/mind/understanding/conscience* |
| אֹהֵב | *one who loves* |
| | Qal Ptcp ms אהב |
| נַפְשׁוֹ | *his soul/life/self* |

שֹׁמֵר תְּבוּנָה לִמְצֹא־טוֹב:

| | |
|---|---|
| שֹׁמֵר | *one who guards/keeps/heeds* |
| | Qal Ptcp ms שמר |
| תְּבוּנָה | *understanding/discernment* |
| לִמְצֹא־ | *to find/discover/gain/obtain* |
| | Qal Inf Cst מצא + prep לְ |
| טוֹב | *good/goodness/benefit* |

# חָכְמַת עָרוּם הָבִין דַּרְכֹּו

| | |
|---|---|
| חָכְמַת עָרוּם | *wisdom of prudent/shrewd/clever person* |
| הָבִין | *to understand/discern/perceive/ comprehend*<br>בין Hiph Inf Cst |
| דַּרְכֹּו | *his way/path* |

# וְאִוֶּלֶת כְּסִילִים מִרְמָה:

| | |
|---|---|
| וְאִוֶּלֶת כְּסִילִים | *but folly of fools/dolts/idiots* |
| מִרְמָה | *deceit/treachery* |

גַּם־לְרֵעֵהוּ יִשָּׂנֵא רָשׁ

גַּם    *even/also*

לְרֵעֵהוּ    *by his neighbor/friend/companion*

יִשָּׂנֵא    *(he) is hated*
     Niph Impf 3ms שׂנא

רָשׁ    *one who is poor*
     Qal Ptcp ms רושׁ

וְאֹהֲבֵי עָשִׁיר רַבִּים׃

וְאֹהֲבֵי    *but ones who love*
     Qal Ptcp mp אהב + conj וְ

עָשִׁיר    *rich person*

רַבִּים    *many*

# תּוֹעֲבַת יְהוָה דֶּרֶךְ רָשָׁע

תּוֹעֲבַת יְהוָה    *abomination of*
                 **YHWH**

דֶּרֶךְ רָשָׁע    *way/path of*
                 *wicked person*

# וּמְרַדֵּף צְדָקָה יֶאֱהָב:

וּמְרַדֵּף    *but one who pursues*
           Piel Ptcp ms רדף + conj וְ

צְדָקָה    *righteousness/truthfulness/justice*

יֶאֱהָב    *he loves*
         Qal Impf 3ms אהב

---

A shrewd man's wisdom lies in perceiving his path,
but the folly of dolts is deceit.

PROV 14:8 ▪ DAY 2

## תַּאֲוַת אָדָם חַסְדּוֹ

| | |
|---|---|
| תַּאֲוַת אָדָם | *desire/longing/appetite of man/person* |
| חַסְדּוֹ | *his lovingkindness/faithfulness/loyalty/ steadfast love/probity/disgrace/shame* |

## וְטוֹב־רָשׁ מֵאִישׁ כָּזָב׃

| | |
|---|---|
| וְטוֹב | *and better* |
| רָשׁ | *one who is poor* |
| | Qal Ptcp ms רוש |
| מֵאִישׁ כָּזָב | *than man/person of lie/falsehood* |

---

A penurious person is resented even by his friend,
but those who dote on an affluent man are many.

PROV 14:20 • DAY 3

דֶּרֶךְ אֱוִיל יָשָׁר בְּעֵינָיו

| | |
|---|---|
| דֶּרֶךְ אֱוִיל | *way/path of* <br> *fool* |
| יָשָׁר | *straight/right/correct/upright* |
| בְּעֵינָיו | *in his eyes* |

וְשֹׁמֵעַ לְעֵצָה חָכָם:

| | |
|---|---|
| וְשֹׁמֵעַ | *but one who listens* <br> וְ conj + שׁמע Qal Ptcp ms |
| לְעֵצָה | *to counsel/advice* |
| חָכָם | *wise/sage* |

The manner of a malevolent man is an abomination to YHWH,
but he cherishes one who pursues piety.

PROV 15:9 ▪ DAY 4

תַּאֲוָה נִהְיָה תֶּעֱרַב לְנָפֶשׁ

| | |
|---|---|
| תַּאֲוָה | *desire/longing* |
| נִהְיָה | *(that which is) accomplished/ (that) which has occurred* |
| | Niph Ptcp fs היה |
| תֶּעֱרַב | *(it) is pleasant/sweet* |
| | Qal Impf 3fs ערב |
| לְנָפֶשׁ | *to/for soul/life/self/appetite/desire* |

וְתוֹעֲבַת כְּסִילִים סוּר מֵרָע:

| | |
|---|---|
| וְתוֹעֲבַת כְּסִילִים | *but abomination of fools/dolts/idiots* |
| סוּר | *to turn away/aside* |
| | Qal Inf Cst סור |
| מֵרָע | *from evil* |

---

A person's longing is for one's loyalty;
indeed, a poor man is better than a perjurer.

PROV 19:22 ▪ DAY 5

# רֹדֵף צְדָקָה וָחָסֶד

| רֹדֵף | *one who pursues* |
|---|---|
| | Qal Ptcp ms רדף |
| צְדָקָה | *righteousness/truthfulness/justice* |
| וָחָסֶד | *and lovingkindness/loyalty/ faithfulness/steadfast love/probity* |

# יִמְצָא חַיִּים צְדָקָה וְכָבוֹד:

| יִמְצָא | *(he) will find/discover/gain/obtain* |
|---|---|
| | Qal Impf 3ms מצא |
| חַיִּים | *life* |
| צְדָקָה | *righteousness/truthfulness/justice/ deliverance* |
| וְכָבוֹד | *and honor/respect/reputation/glory* |

---

A dimwit's way is right in his eyes,
but an insightful man heeds advice.

PROV 12:15 ▪ DAY 6

אָדָם עָרוּם כֹּסֶה דָּעַת

| | |
|---|---|
| אָדָם | *man/person* |
| עָרוּם | *prudent/shrewd/clever* |
| כֹּסֶה | *(one who) conceals* |
| | Qal Ptcp ms כסה |
| דָּעַת | *knowledge* |

וְלֵב כְּסִילִים יִקְרָא אִוֶּלֶת:

| | |
|---|---|
| וְלֵב כְּסִילִים | *but heart/mind of fools/dolts/idiots* |
| יִקְרָא | *(it) proclaims* |
| | Qal Impf 3ms קרא |
| אִוֶּלֶת | *folly* |

---

A desire fulfilled is dulcet to the soul,
but for imbeciles it is anathema to turn away from evil.

PROV 13:19 ▪ DAY 7

יֵשׁ דֶּרֶךְ יָשָׁר לִפְנֵי־אִישׁ

| יֵשׁ | *there is* |
| דֶּרֶךְ | *way/path* |
| יָשָׁר | *right/straight/correct/upright* |
| לִפְנֵי־אִישׁ | *before man/person* |

וְאַחֲרִיתָהּ דַּרְכֵי־מָוֶת:

| וְאַחֲרִיתָהּ | *but its end/future* |
| דַּרְכֵי־מָוֶת | *ways/paths of death* |

פִּי־כְסִיל מְחִתָּה־לֹו

| | |
|---|---|
| פִּי־כְסִיל | *mouth of*<br>*fool/dolt/idiot* |
| מְחִתָּה | *ruin* |
| לֹו | *to him* |

וּשְׂפָתָיו מוֹקֵשׁ נַפְשֹׁו:

| | |
|---|---|
| וּשְׂפָתָיו | *and his lips* |
| מוֹקֵשׁ נַפְשֹׁו | *snare/trap of*<br>*his soul/life/self* |

---

A smart man keeps his knowledge to himself,
but dolts' hearts spout drivel.

PROV 12:23 ▪ DAY 9

מִפְּרִי פִי־אִישׁ תִּשְׂבַּע בִּטְנוֹ

מִפְּרִי פִי־אִישׁ

*from fruit of*
*mouth of*
*man/person*

תִּשְׂבַּע

*(it) will be satisfied/satiated/full*

Qal Impf 3fs שׂבע

בִּטְנוֹ

*his stomach/belly*

תְּבוּאַת שְׂפָתָיו יִשְׂבָּע:

תְּבוּאַת שְׂפָתָיו

*produce/yield of*
*his lips*

יִשְׂבָּע

*he will be satisfied/satiated/full*

Qal Impf 3ms שׂבע

---

There's a path that seems perfect to a person,
but it ends up being a passage to perdition.

PROV 14:12 ▪ DAY 10

# מַצִּיל נְפָשׁוֹת עֵד אֱמֶת

מַצִּיל    *(one who/that) delivers/rescues/saves*

נצל Hiph Ptcp ms

נְפָשׁוֹת    *lives/persons*

עֵד אֱמֶת    *witness/testimony of*
        *truth/honesty/trustworthiness/*
        *faithfulness*

# וְיָפִחַ כְּזָבִים מִרְמָה:

וְיָפִחַ    *but witness of*

וְ + יָפִיחַ noun

     *but he breathes out/pours out*

וְ + פוח Hiph Impf 3ms

כְּזָבִים    *lies/falsehoods*

מִרְמָה    *deceit/treachery*

---

A numbskull's mouth is his ruin,
and his lips are a trap for his life.

PROV 18:7 ▪ DAY 11

## רְצוֹן־מֶלֶךְ לְעֶבֶד מַשְׂכִּיל

רְצוֹן־מֶלֶךְ     *favor/delight/desire of
king/ruler*

לְעֶבֶד     *to/on/toward servant/slave*

מַשְׂכִּיל     *(one) who acts prudently/wisely/with
understanding*

Hiph Ptcp ms שׂכל


## וְעֶבְרָתוֹ תִּהְיֶה מֵבִישׁ:

וְעֶבְרָתוֹ     *but his wrath/rage/anger/fury*

תִּהְיֶה     *(it) will be*

Qal Impf 3fs היה

מֵבִישׁ     *one who acts shamefully/causes shame*

Hiph Ptcp ms בושׁ


---

A person's paunch will be full from his mouth's fruit;
he'll be satiated by his lips' produce.

PROV 18:20 • DAY 12

מְקוֹר חַיִּים פִּי צַדִּיק

מְקוֹר חַיִּים    *fountain/spring/source of life*

פִּי צַדִּיק    *mouth of righteous person*

וּפִי רְשָׁעִים יְכַסֶּה חָמָס:

וּפִי רְשָׁעִים    *but mouth of wicked people*

יְכַסֶּה    *(it) conceals/covers up*
כסה Piel Impf 3ms

חָמָס    *violence*

---

Truthful testimony saves lives,
but a treacherous person pours out perjury.

PROV 14:25 ▪ DAY 13

## תַּאֲוַת צַדִּיקִים אַךְ־טֽוֹב

תַּאֲוַת צַדִּיקִים　　*desire/longing/expectation of*
　　　　　　　　　　　*righteous people*

אַךְ־　　*surely/indeed/only*

טֽוֹב　　*good/goodness/benefit*

## תִּקְוַת רְשָׁעִים עֶבְרָֽה׃

תִּקְוַת רְשָׁעִים　　*hope of*
　　　　　　　　　　*wicked people*

עֶבְרָֽה　　*wrath/rage/anger/fury*

---

A ruler is favorable toward a sage slave,
but his fury falls on one whose actions are untoward.

PROV 14:35 • DAY 14

## מַשְׂכִּיל צַדִּיק לְבֵית רָשָׁע

| | |
|---|---|
| מַשְׂכִּיל | *(one who) acts prudently/wisely/ with understanding* |
| | Hiph Ptcp ms שׂכל |
| צַדִּיק | *righteous person* |
| לְבֵית רָשָׁע | *toward/with regard to house/household/family of wicked person* |

## מְסַלֵּף רְשָׁעִים לָרָע:

| | |
|---|---|
| מְסַלֵּף | *(one who) overthrows/ruins/subverts* |
| | Piel Ptcp ms סלף |
| רְשָׁעִים | *wicked people* |
| לָרָע | *to/for the evil/harm/calamity* |

---

A just man's mouth is a vivifying fountain,
but the mouth of evildoers covers up violence.

PROV 10:11 ▪ DAY 15

## טוֹב־רָשׁ הוֹלֵךְ בְּתֻמּוֹ

טוֹב־    *better*

רָשׁ    *one who is poor*
     Qal Ptcp ms רושׁ

הוֹלֵךְ    *(one) who walks*
     Qal Ptcp ms הלך

בְּתֻמּוֹ    *in his integrity/innocence/*
     *blamelessness/purity/perfection*

## מֵעִקֵּשׁ שְׂפָתָיו וְהוּא כְסִיל׃

מֵעִקֵּשׁ שְׂפָתָיו    *than one perverse/crooked/twisted of*
     *his lips*

וְהוּא    *and he/that one*

כְסִיל    *fool/dolt/idiot*

---

The yearning of the godly is solely for good;
the aspiration of the ignoble is wrath.

PROV 11:23 ▪ DAY 16

## לֵב נָבוֹן יִקְנֶה־דָּעַת

| | |
|---|---|
| לֵב נָבוֹן | *heart/mind of* |
| | *one who is understanding/discerning/* |
| | *perceptive/intelligent* |
| | Niph Ptcp ms בין |
| יִקְנֶה־ | *(it) acquires/gets/gains/obtains* |
| | Qal Impf 3ms קנה |
| דָּעַת | *knowledge* |

## וְאֹזֶן חֲכָמִים תְּבַקֶּשׁ־דָּעַת:

| | |
|---|---|
| וְאֹזֶן חֲכָמִים | *and ear of* |
| | *wise/sage people* |
| תְּבַקֶּשׁ־ | *(it) seeks* |
| | Piel Impf 3fs בקשׁ |
| דָּעַת | *knowledge* |

---

A virtuous man acts shrewdly concerning a vile man's house,
subverting the sinister for evil.

PROV 21:12 ▪ DAY 17

# עֵינֵי יְהוָה נָצְרוּ דָעַת

| | |
|---|---|
| עֵינֵי יְהוָה | *eyes of*<br>**YHWH** |
| נָצְרוּ | *(they) guarded/protected/preserved*<br>Qal Pf 3cp נצר |
| דָעַת | *knowledge* |

# וַיְסַלֵּף דִּבְרֵי בֹגֵד׃

| | |
|---|---|
| וַיְסַלֵּף | *then he overthrew/ruined/subverted*<br>Piel wayyiqtol 3ms סלף |
| דִּבְרֵי בֹגֵד | *words of*<br>*one who is treacherous*<br>Qal Ptcp ms בגד |

---

Better an impecunious individual who walks in innocence
than a man of warped lips; indeed, the latter is a lout.

PROV 19:1 ▪ DAY 18

# עֲשֹׂה צְדָקָה וּמִשְׁפָּט

עֲשֹׂה    *to do/practice/execute*
Qal Inf Cst עשׂה

צְדָקָה    *righteousness/truthfulness/justice*

וּמִשְׁפָּט    *and justice*

# נִבְחָר לַיהוָה מִזָּבַח:

נִבְחָר    *(it) is preferable*
Niph Ptcp ms בחר

לַיהוָה    *to YHWH*

מִזָּבַח    *to/more than/instead of sacrifice*

---

An astute mind attains awareness,
and the ear of the sagacious seeks enlightenment.

PROV 18:15 ▪ DAY 19

## שֹׁמֵר פִּיו וּלְשׁוֹנֹו

| שֹׁמֵר | *one who guards/keeps/watches* |
|---|---|
| | Qal Ptcp ms שמר |
| פִּיו | *his mouth* |
| וּלְשׁוֹנֹו | *and his tongue* |

## שֹׁמֵר מִצָּרֹות נַפְשֹׁו:

| שֹׁמֵר | *one who guards/keeps/preserves/ protects* |
|---|---|
| | Qal Ptcp ms שמר |
| מִצָּרֹות | *from troubles/distresses* |
| נַפְשֹׁו | *his soul/life/self* |

---

YHWH's eyes preserved knowledge,
and he subverted the perfidious person's words.

PROV 22:12 ▪ DAY 20

עֲטֶרֶת חֲכָמִים עָשְׁרָם

| | |
|---|---|
| עֲטֶרֶת חֲכָמִים | *crown of*<br>*wise/sage people* |
| עָשְׁרָם | *their wealth* |

אִוֶּלֶת כְּסִילִים אִוֶּלֶת:

| | |
|---|---|
| אִוֶּלֶת כְּסִילִים | *folly of*<br>*fools/dolts/idiots* |
| אִוֶּלֶת | *folly* |

Practicing righteousness and justice
is YHWH's preference over sacrifice.

PROV 21:3 ▪ DAY 21

## יֵשׁ מִתְעַשֵּׁר וְאֵין כֹּל

| | |
|---|---|
| יֵשׁ | *there is* |
| מִתְעַשֵּׁר | *one who pretends to be rich/considers himself rich*<br>Hith Ptcp ms עשׁר |
| וְאֵין | *but there is not* |
| כֹּל | *everything/anything* |

## מִתְרוֹשֵׁשׁ וְהוֹן רָב:

| | |
|---|---|
| מִתְרוֹשֵׁשׁ | *one who pretends to be poor/considers himself poor*<br>Hithpolel Ptcp ms רושׁ |
| וְהוֹן | *but wealth* |
| רָב | *much/great/abundant* |

---

He who watches his mouth and his tongue
preserves himself from adversities.

PROV 21:23 ▪ DAY 22

## נִבְחָר שֵׁם מֵעֹשֶׁר רָב

| | |
|---|---|
| נִבְחָר | *(it) is preferable* |
| | Niph Ptcp ms בחר |
| שֵׁם | *name* |
| מֵעֹשֶׁר | *to/more than/instead of wealth* |
| רָב | *much/great/abundant* |

## מִכֶּסֶף וּמִזָּהָב חֵן טוֹב:

| | |
|---|---|
| מִכֶּסֶף | *more than silver* |
| וּמִזָּהָב | *and more than gold* |
| חֵן | *favor/grace* |
| טוֹב | *good* |

---

The crown of the wise is their wealth;
the folly of dolts is folly.

PROV 14:24 ▪ DAY 23

מְקוֹר חַיִּים שֵׂכֶל בְּעָלָיו

| | |
|---|---|
| מְקוֹר חַיִּים | *fountain/spring/source of life* |
| שֵׂכֶל בְּעָלָיו | *prudence/wisdom/understanding of its possessor/owner* |

וּמוּסַר אֱוִלִים אִוֶּלֶת׃

| | |
|---|---|
| וּמוּסַר אֱוִלִים | *but instruction/training/discipline/ correction/chastisement/warning of fools* |
| אִוֶּלֶת | *folly* |

There's one who thinks himself rich, though he has nothing—
another who considers himself poor, though he has vast wealth.

PROV 13:7 ▪ DAY 24

מָ֫וֶת וְחַיִּים בְּיַד־לָשׁוֹן

| | |
|--:|:--|
| מָ֫וֶת | *death* |
| וְחַיִּים | *and life* |
| בְּיַד־לָשׁוֹן | *in hand/power/control of tongue* |

וְאֹהֲבֶ֫יהָ יֹאכַל פִּרְיָהּ׃

| | |
|--:|:--|
| וְאֹהֲבֶ֫יהָ | *and ones who love it*<br>Qal Ptcp אהב mp + 3fs sx + conj וְ |
| יֹאכַל | *(he) eats*<br>Qal Impf 3ms(!) אכל |
| פִּרְיָהּ | *its fruit* |

---

Reputation is preferable to great riches;
good grace, to silver and gold.

PROV 22:1 ▪ DAY 25

לֵ֣ב נָ֭בוֹן יְבַקֶּשׁ־דָּ֑עַת

לֵ֣ב נָ֭בוֹן  *heart/mind of*
*one who is understanding/discerning/*
*perceptive/intelligent*

Niph Ptcp ms בין

יְבַקֶּשׁ־  *(it) seeks*

Piel Impf 3ms בקשׁ

דָּ֑עַת  *knowledge*

וּפִ֖י כְסִילִ֣ים יִרְעֶ֣ה אִוֶּֽלֶת׃

וּפִ֖י כְסִילִ֣ים  *but mouth of*
*fools/dolts/idiots*

וּפני כְסִילִ֣ים  KETIV

יִרְעֶ֣ה  *(it) feeds/grazes on*

Qal Impf 3ms רעה

אִוֶּֽלֶת  *folly*

---

Prudence is an invigorating spring to its possessor,
but the instruction of the inept is idiocy.

PROV 16:22 ▪ DAY 26

# שְׂאֵת פְּנֵי־רָשָׁע לֹא־טֹוב

שְׂאֵת     *to lift up/bear*
Qal Inf Cst נשׂא

פְּנֵי־רָשָׁע     *face of*
*wicked/guilty person*

לֹא־     *not*

טֹוב     *good*

# לְהַטֹּות צַדִּיק בַּמִּשְׁפָּט:

לְהַטֹּות     *to turn away/aside*
Hiph Inf Cst נטה + prep לְ

צַדִּיק     *righteous person*

בַּמִּשְׁפָּט     *in the judgment/from the justice*

---

Death and life are in the tongue's hand,
and those who love it eat its fruit.

PROV 18:21 • DAY 27

## כֹּל פָּעַל יְהוָה לַמַּעֲנֵהוּ

| | |
|---|---|
| כֹּל | *everything* |
| פָּעַל | *(he) made/created* |
| | פעל Qal Pf 3ms |
| יְהוָה | **YHWH** |
| לַמַּעֲנֵהוּ | *for its/his purpose* |

## וְגַם־רָשָׁע לְיוֹם רָעָה:

| | |
|---|---|
| וְגַם־ | *and also/even* |
| רָשָׁע | *wicked person* |
| לְיוֹם רָעָה | *for day of* |
| | *evil/harm/trouble/calamity/disaster* |

---

A discerning man's mind craves knowledge,
but the mouth of ignoramuses grazes on irrationality.

PROV 15:14 ▪ DAY 28

כֶּסֶף נִבְחָר לְשׁוֹן צַדִּיק

| | |
|---|---|
| כֶּסֶף | *silver* |
| נִבְחָר | *(that which is) tested/refined/chosen* |
| | Niph Ptcp ms בחר |
| לְשׁוֹן צַדִּיק | *tongue of* |
| | *righteous person* |

לֵב רְשָׁעִים כִּמְעָט:

| | |
|---|---|
| לֵב רְשָׁעִים | *heart/mind/understanding of* |
| | *wicked people* |
| כִּמְעָט | *as/like little* |

---

It's unacceptable to show a guilty person partiality,
to turn an innocent one away from justice.

PROV 18:5 ▪ DAY 29

שִׂפְתֵי חֲכָמִים יְזָרוּ דָעַת

| | |
|---|---|
| שִׂפְתֵי חֲכָמִים | *lips of* |
| | *wise/sage people* |
| יְזָרוּ | *(they) spread/winnow* |
| | Piel Impf 3mp זרה |
| דָעַת | *knowledge* |

וְלֵב כְּסִילִים לֹא־כֵן:

| | |
|---|---|
| וְלֵב כְּסִילִים | *but heart/mind of* |
| | *fools/dolts/idiots* |
| לֹא־ | *not* |
| כֵן | *so/thus* |

YHWH created everything for his purpose,
including a depraved person for a day of disaster.

PROV 16:4 ▪ DAY 30

מִפְּרִי פִי־אִישׁ יֹאכַל טֹוב

| | |
|---:|:---|
| מִפְּרִי פִי־אִישׁ | *from fruit of* <br> *mouth of* <br> *man/person* |
| יֹאכַל | *he will eat* <br> אכל Qal Impf 3ms |
| טֹוב | *good/goodness/benefit/well* |

וְנֶפֶשׁ בֹּגְדִים חָמָס׃

| | |
|---:|:---|
| וְנֶפֶשׁ בֹּגְדִים | *but desire/appetite/soul/life of* <br> *ones who are treacherous* <br> בגד Qal Ptcp mp |
| חָמָס | *violence* |

---

A virtuous man's tongue is refined silver;
the heart of the wicked is worthless.

PROV 10:20 ▪ DAY 31

לֵךְ מִנֶּגֶד לְאִישׁ כְּסִיל

| | |
|---|---|
| לֵךְ | *go* |
| | Qal Impv ms הלך |
| מִנֶּגֶד לְאִישׁ | *from presence of man/person* |
| כְּסִיל | *foolish/stupid* |

וּבַל־יָדַעְתָּ שִׂפְתֵי־דָעַת׃

| | |
|---|---|
| וּבַל־יָדַעְתָּ | *and/because/when you did not know* |
| | Qal Pf 2ms ידע |
| שִׂפְתֵי־דָעַת | *lips of*<br>*knowledge* |

---

Sages' lips spread erudition,
but dolts' hearts—not so.

PROV 15:7 ▪ DAY 32

נֶפֶשׁ רָשָׁע אִוְּתָה־רָע

| נֶפֶשׁ רָשָׁע | soul/appetite of wicked person |
| אִוְּתָה־ | (it) desires/longs for |
| | Piel Pf 3fs אוה |
| רָע | evil/harm |

לֹא־יֻחַן בְּעֵינָיו רֵעֵהוּ׃

| לֹא־יֻחַן | (he) is not shown favor/mercy/pity |
| | Hoph Impf 3ms חנן |
| בְּעֵינָיו | in his eyes |
| רֵעֵהוּ | his neighbor/companion/friend |

---

From a man's mouth's fruit will he eat well,
but the craving of the virulent is for violence.

PROV 13:2 ▪ DAY 33

לְשׁוֹן חֲכָמִים תֵּיטִיב דָּעַת

| | |
|---:|:---|
| לְשׁוֹן חֲכָמִים | *tongue of* *wise/sage people* |
| תֵּיטִיב | *(it) makes good/makes better/adorns* Hiph Impf 3fs יטב |
| דָּעַת | *knowledge* |

וּפִי כְסִילִים יַבִּיעַ אִוֶּלֶת:

| | |
|---:|:---|
| וּפִי כְסִילִים | *but mouth of* *fools/dolts/idiots* |
| יַבִּיעַ | *(it) spews/pours forth* Hiph Impf 3ms נבע |
| אִוֶּלֶת | *folly* |

---

Leave a dunce's presence
as soon as you don't detect perceptive lips.

PROV 14:7 ▪ DAY 34

# מַשְׂכִּיל עַל־דָּבָר יִמְצָא־טוֹב

| | |
|---|---|
| מַשְׂכִּיל | *one who acts prudently/wisely/with understanding* |
| | Hiph Ptcp ms שׂכל |
| עַל־דָּבָר | *concerning word/matter/affair* |
| יִמְצָא־ | *(he) will find/discover/gain/obtain* |
| | Qal Impf 3ms מצא |
| טוֹב | *good/goodness/benefit* |

# וּבוֹטֵחַ בַּיהוָה אַשְׁרָיו:

| | |
|---|---|
| וּבוֹטֵחַ | *and one who trusts/is confident/is secure* |
| | Qal Ptcp ms בטח + conj וְ |
| בַּיהוָה | *in YHWH* |
| אַשְׁרָיו | *blessed/happy is he* |

---

A hoodlum's soul hankers after harm;
his companion gets no compassion in his sight.

PROV 21:10 ▪ DAY 35

## אֹהֵב טְהָר־לֵב

אֹהֵב     *one who loves*

       Qal Ptcp ms אהב

טְהָר־לֵב     *pure/clean of*
              *heart/mind/conscience*

       KETIV טהור־לֵב

## חֵן שְׂפָתָיו רֵעֵהוּ מֶלֶךְ׃

חֵן     *favor/grace/elegance*

שְׂפָתָיו     *his lips*

רֵעֵהוּ     *his friend/companion*

מֶלֶךְ     *king/ruler*

---

The tongue of the learned adorns knowledge,
but the mouth of the stupid spews forth folly.

PROV 15:2 ▪ DAY 36

פְּרִי־צַדִּיק עֵץ חַיִּים

| | |
|---|---|
| פְּרִי־צַדִּיק | *fruit of* |
| | *righteous person* |
| עֵץ חַיִּים | *tree of* |
| | *life* |

וְלֹקֵחַ נְפָשׁוֹת חָכָם:

| | |
|---|---|
| וְלֹקֵחַ | *and one who takes/receives/acquires* |
| | Qal Ptcp לקח ms + conj וְ |
| נְפָשׁוֹת | *persons/lives/souls* |
| חָכָם | *wise/sage* |

.

---

One who acts sensibly in a matter obtains good,
and one who trusts in YHWH—blessed is he!

PROV 16:20 • DAY 37

# בָּז־לְרֵעֵהוּ חֲסַר־לֵב

| | |
|---|---|
| בָּז־ | *one who despises* |
| | Qal Ptcp ms בוז |
| לְרֵעֵהוּ | *his neighbor/friend/companion* |
| חֲסַר־לֵב | *lacking/devoid of heart/mind/understanding/ conscience* |

# וְאִישׁ תְּבוּנוֹת יַחֲרִישׁ:

| | |
|---|---|
| וְאִישׁ תְּבוּנוֹת | *but man/person of understandings/discernments* |
| יַחֲרִישׁ | *(he) is silent/quiet // (he) keeps silent/ quiet // (he) holds his peace* |
| | Hiph Impf 3ms חרשׁ |

---

He who prioritizes purity of heart—
his lips are elegance; the king will be his companion.

PROV 22:11 ▪ DAY 38

## מַחְשְׁבוֹת צַדִּיקִים מִשְׁפָּט

מַחְשְׁבוֹת צַדִּיקִים　*thoughts/plans of righteous people*

מִשְׁפָּט　*justice*

## תַּחְבֻּלוֹת רְשָׁעִים מִרְמָה׃

תַּחְבֻּלוֹת רְשָׁעִים　*counsels/guidance of wicked people*

מִרְמָה　*deceit/treachery*

---

A virtuous man's fruit is a tree of life,
and one who takes souls is wise.

PROV 11:30 ▪ DAY 39

עֹכֵר בֵּיתוֹ יִנְחַל־רוּחַ

עֹכֵר     *one who troubles*
       Qal Ptcp ms עכר

בֵּיתוֹ     *his house/household/family*

יִנְחַל־     *(he) will inherit*
       Qal Impf 3ms נחל

רוּחַ     *wind*

וְעֶבֶד אֱוִיל לַחֲכַם־לֵב:

וְעֶבֶד     *and servant/slave*

אֱוִיל     *fool*

לַחֲכַם־לֵב     *to one wise/sage of
heart/mind*

---

He who disrespects his friend is devoid of heart,
but a man of acumen keeps quiet.

PROV 11:12 ▪ DAY 40

## בְּפֶשַׁע שְׂפָתַיִם מוֹקֵשׁ רָע

בְּפֶשַׁע שְׂפָתַיִם     *in transgression/offense of lips*

מוֹקֵשׁ רָע     *snare/trap of evil/bad person*

## וַיֵּצֵא מִצָּרָה צַדִּיק:

וַיֵּצֵא     *but (he) came out*
Qal wayyiqtol 3ms יצא

מִצָּרָה     *of/from trouble/distress*

צַדִּיק     *righteous person*

---

The intentions of the impartial are just;
the counsels of the corrupt are treasonous.

PROV 12:5 ▪ DAY 41

תּוֹחֶלֶת צַדִּיקִים שִׂמְחָה

תּוֹחֶלֶת צַדִּיקִים    *hope/expectation of righteous people*

שִׂמְחָה    *joy/gladness/happiness/pleasure/mirth*

וְתִקְוַת רְשָׁעִים תֹּאבֵד:

וְתִקְוַת רְשָׁעִים    *but hope of wicked people*

תֹּאבֵד    *(it) perishes/is destroyed*

Qal Impf 3fs אבד

---

He who afflicts his family will inherit wind,
and a half-wit is a slave to a wise-hearted man.

PROV 11:29 ▪ DAY 42

## יִרְאַ֣ת יְהֹוָ֣ה מוּסַ֣ר חׇכְמָ֑ה

יִרְאַ֣ת יְהֹוָ֣ה    *fear/awe/reverence of*
                      **YHWH**

מוּסַ֣ר חׇכְמָ֑ה    *instruction/training/education/warning/*
                      *discipline/correction/chastisement of*
                      *wisdom*

## וְלִפְנֵ֖י כָב֣וֹד עֲנָוָֽה׃

וְלִפְנֵ֖י כָב֣וֹד    *and before honor/respect/reputation/*
                      *glory*

עֲנָוָֽה    *humility/meekness*

---

A truculent man gets trapped by his transgressing lips,
but a virtuous man exited from trouble.

PROV 12:13 ▪ DAY 43

גַּם עֲנוֹשׁ לַצַּדִּיק לֹא־טוֹב

| | |
|---|---|
| גַּם | *also/likewise/both* |
| עֲנוֹשׁ | *to punish/impose a fine*<br>Qal Inf Cst עבשׁ |
| לַצַּדִּיק | *(on) the righteous person* |
| לֹא־ | *not* |
| טוֹב | *good* |

לְהַכּוֹת נְדִיבִים עַל־יֹשֶׁר׃

| | |
|---|---|
| לְהַכּוֹת | *to strike*<br>לְ prep + נכה Hiph Inf Cst |
| נְדִיבִים | *generous people/nobles* |
| עַל־יֹשֶׁר | *on account of uprightness/integrity* |

---

The hope of the honorable is happiness,
but the aspiration of the heinous perishes.

PROV 10:28 · DAY 44

## בַּיִת וָהוֹן נַחֲלַת אָבוֹת

בַּיִת     *house/household/home/family/dynasty*

וָהוֹן     *and wealth*

נַחֲלַת אָבוֹת     *inheritance of*
           *fathers/parents/forebears*


## וּמֵיהוָה אִשָּׁה מַשְׂכָּלֶת:

וּמֵיהוָה     *and/but from* YHWH

אִשָּׁה     *woman/wife*

מַשְׂכָּלֶת     *(one) who acts wisely/prudently/with*
      *understanding*
          Hiph Ptcp fs שׂכל


---

Awe of YHWH is wisdom's instruction,
and abasement precedes honor.

PROV 15:33 ▪ DAY 45

# תַּאֲוַת עָצֵל תְּמִיתֶנּוּ

| תַּאֲוַת עָצֵל | *desire/appetite of lazy/sluggish/slothful person* |
|---|---|
| תְּמִיתֶנּוּ | *(it) kills him* |
| | Hiph Impf 3fs מות + 3ms sx |

# כִּי־מֵאֲנוּ יָדָיו לַעֲשׂוֹת:

| כִּי־ | *for/because* |
|---|---|
| מֵאֲנוּ | *(they) refuse* |
| | Piel Pf 3cp מאן |
| יָדָיו | *his hands* |
| לַעֲשׂוֹת | *to act/work* |
| | Qal Inf Cst עשׂה + prep לְ |

---

Penalizing a righteous person is problematic;
likewise, attacking an altruistic man for his uprightness.

PROV 17:26 ▪ DAY 46

כָּל־הַיּוֹם הִתְאַוָּה תַאֲוָה

כָּל־הַיּוֹם     *all the day*

הִתְאַוָּה     *he continually desires*

        Hith Pf 3ms אוה

תַאֲוָה     *desire*

וְצַדִּיק יִתֵּן וְלֹא יַחְשֹׂךְ:

וְצַדִּיק     *but righteous person*

יִתֵּן     *(he) gives*

        Qal Impf 3ms נתן

וְלֹא יַחְשֹׂךְ     *and (he) does not withhold/hold back*

        Qal Impf 3ms חשׂך

---

A family and a fortune are one's parents' bequest,
but a wise wife is from YHWH.

PROV 19:14 ▪ DAY 47

## בֵּן חָכָם יְשַׂמַּח־אָב

בֵּן    *son/child*

חָכָם    *wise/sage*

יְשַׂמַּח־    *(he/it) makes joyful/glad/happy*
      Piel Impf 3ms שׂמח

אָב    *father*

## וּבֵן כְּסִיל תּוּגַת אִמּוֹ:

וּבֵן    *but son/child*

כְּסִיל    *foolish/stupid*

תּוּגַת אִמּוֹ    *grief/sorrow of his/its mother*

---

A sluggard's desire slays him,
since his hands are unwilling to work.

PROV 21:25 ▪ DAY 48

רַב־אָדָ֗ם יִ֭קְרָא אִ֣ישׁ חַסְדּ֑וֹ

| | |
|---:|:---|
| רַב־אָדָ֗ם | *abundance/multitude of humankind/humanity* |
| יִ֭קְרָא | *(he/it) proclaims* <br> Qal Impf 3ms קרא |
| אִ֣ישׁ | *man/person/each* |
| חַסְדּ֑וֹ | *his lovingkindness/faithfulness/loyalty/ steadfast love/probity* |

וְאִ֥ישׁ אֱ֝מוּנִ֗ים מִ֣י יִמְצָֽא׃

| | |
|---:|:---|
| וְאִ֥ישׁ אֱ֝מוּנִ֗ים | *but man/person of faithfulnesses/honesties* |
| מִ֣י | *who?* |
| יִמְצָֽא | *(he) will find* <br> Qal Impf 3ms מצא |

---

He longingly lusts all day long,
but a good man gives and isn't stingy.

PROV 21:26 ▪ DAY 49

# שִׂמְחָה לַצַּדִּיק עֲשׂוֹת מִשְׁפָּט

שִׂמְחָה    *joy/gladness/happiness/pleasure/mirth*

לַצַּדִּיק    *to/for the righteous person*

עֲשׂוֹת    *to do/practice/execute*
       Qal Inf Cst עשׂה

מִשְׁפָּט    *justice/judgment*

# וּמְחִתָּה לְפֹעֲלֵי אָוֶן:

וּמְחִתָּה    *but terror/ruin*

לְפֹעֲלֵי    *to/for ones who work/practice*
       Qal Ptcp mp פעל + prep לְ

אָוֶן    *iniquity/injustice/sin/evil*

---

A sagacious son brings delight to his dad,
but a churlish child is his mom's misery.

PROV 10:1 ▪ DAY 50

## אֵין חָכְמָה וְאֵין תְּבוּנָה

| | |
|---:|:---|
| אֵין | *there is not* |
| חָכְמָה | *wisdom* |
| וְאֵין | *and there is not* |
| תְּבוּנָה | *understanding/discernment* |

## וְאֵין עֵצָה לְנֶגֶד יְהוָה:

| | |
|---:|:---|
| וְאֵין | *and there is not* |
| עֵצָה | *counsel/advice/plan/plot* |
| לְנֶגֶד יְהוָה | *before/in front of/against* YHWH |

---

The preponderance of people say they're steadfast,
but who can find someone who is, in fact, faithful?

PROV 20:6 ▪ DAY 51

## בֵּן חָכָם מוּסַר אָב

| בֵּן | son/child |
|---|---|
| חָכָם | wise/sage |
| מוּסַר אָב | instruction/training/education/warning/ discipline/correction/chastisement of father/parent |

## וְלֵץ לֹא־שָׁמַע גְּעָרָה:

| וְלֵץ | but scoffer/scorner/mocker |
|---|---|
| לֹא־שָׁמַע | (he) does not hear/listen to/heed |
| | Qal Pf 3ms שׁמע |
| גְּעָרָה | rebuke |

A righteous person takes joy in executing justice,
but this spells doom for evildoers.

PROV 21:15 ▪ DAY 52

מִתְהַלֵּךְ בְּתֻמּוֹ צַדִּיק

| מִתְהַלֵּךְ | (one who) habitually/continually walks |
|---|---|
| | Hith Ptcp ms הלך |
| בְּתֻמּוֹ | in his integrity/innocence/ blamelessness/purity/perfection |
| צַדִּיק | righteous person |

אַשְׁרֵי בָנָיו אַחֲרָיו:

| אַשְׁרֵי | blessed/happy |
|---|---|
| בָנָיו | his children |
| אַחֲרָיו | after him |

There's no wisdom, no understanding,
no plot that can thwart YHWH.

PROV 21:30 ▪ DAY 53

# הוֹלֵךְ אֶת־חֲכָמִים יֶחְכָּם

| | |
|---|---|
| הוֹלֵךְ | *one who walks* |
| | Qal Ptcp ms הלך |
| | KETIV הלוך |
| אֶת־חֲכָמִים | *with wise/sage people* |
| יֶחְכָּם | *(he) is/becomes wise/sage* |
| | Qal Impf 3ms חכם |
| | KETIV וחכם |

# וְרֹעֶה כְסִילִים יֵרוֹעַ:

| | |
|---|---|
| וְרֹעֶה | *but one who is a friend/companion of //*<br>*but one who shepherds/leads* |
| | Qal Ptcp ms רעה + conj וְ |
| כְסִילִים | *fools/dolts/idiots* |
| יֵרוֹעַ | *(he) will suffer evil/harm/calamity* |
| | Niph Impf 3ms רעע |

---

A parent's discipline produces a sagacious son,
but an insolent one won't listen to admonishment.

PROV 13:1 ▪ DAY 54

## תּוֹעֲבַת מְלָכִים עֲשׂוֹת רֶשַׁע

| | |
|---:|:---|
| תּוֹעֲבַת מְלָכִים | *abomination of kings/rulers* |
| עֲשׂוֹת | *to do/practice*<br>Qal Inf Cst עשׂה |
| רֶשַׁע | *wickedness* |

## כִּי בִצְדָקָה יִכּוֹן כִּסֵּא:

| | |
|---:|:---|
| כִּי | *for/because* |
| בִּצְדָקָה | *in/by/through righteousness/ truthfulness/justice* |
| יִכּוֹן | *(it) will be established/secure*<br>Niph Impf 3ms כון |
| כִּסֵּא | *throne* |

---

A saintly man constantly conducts himself with integrity;
his offspring after him will be well off.

PROV 20:7 • DAY 55

בַּעְנָשׁ־לֵץ יֶחְכַּם־פֶּתִי

| | |
|---|---|
| בַּעְנָשׁ־לֵץ | *in/by/through punishing of scoffer/scorner/mocker* |
| | Qal Inf Cst עֲנָשׁ + prep בְּ |
| יֶחְכַּם־ | *(he) becomes wise/sage* |
| | Qal Impf 3ms חכם |
| פֶּתִי | *simpleminded/naïve/ignorant person* |

וּבְהַשְׂכִּיל לְחָכָם יִקַּח־דָּעַת:

| | |
|---|---|
| וּבְהַשְׂכִּיל | *and in teaching // and in acting prudently/wisely/with understanding* |
| | Hiph Inf Cst שׂכל + prep בְּ + conj וְ |
| לְחָכָם | *(toward) wise/sage person* |
| יִקַּח־ | *he acquires/receives* |
| | Qal Impf 3ms לקח |
| דָּעַת | *knowledge* |

---

One who walks with the wise will be enlightened,
but a friend of fools will suffer affliction.

PROV 13:20 ▪ DAY 56

שֹׁמֵר מִצְוָה שֹׁמֵר נַפְשׁוֹ

| שֹׁמֵר | one who keeps/guards/heeds/observes |
|---|---|
| | Qal Ptcp ms שׁמר |

| מִצְוָה | command/commandment/precept |
|---|---|

| שֹׁמֵר | one who guards/keeps/preserves/protects |
|---|---|
| | Qal Ptcp ms שׁמר |

| נַפְשׁוֹ | his soul/life/self |
|---|---|

בּוֹזֵה דְרָכָיו יָמוּת:

| בּוֹזֵה | one who despises |
|---|---|
| | Qal Ptcp ms בזה |

| דְרָכָיו | his ways/paths |
|---|---|

| יָמוּת | (he) will die |
|---|---|
| | Qal Impf 3ms מות |
| | KETIV יומת |

---

Engaging in crimes is reprehensible to rulers,
for through morality is one's throne secure.

PROV 16:12 ▪ DAY 57

## שֹׁחַד מֵחֵיק רָשָׁע יִקָּח

| שֹׁחַד | *bribe* |
|---|---|
| מֵחֵיק | *from bosom* |
| רָשָׁע | *wicked person* |
| יִקָּח | *(he) takes/receives/accepts* |
| | Qal Impf 3ms לקח |

## לְהַטּוֹת אָרְחוֹת מִשְׁפָּט:

| לְהַטּוֹת | *to turn aside/divert* |
|---|---|
| | Hiph Inf Cst נטה + prep לְ |
| אָרְחוֹת מִשְׁפָּט | *ways/paths of justice* |

---

A simpleton becomes sage when a scorner is scourged,
and it's through teaching a sage that he gets insight.

PROV 21:11 ▪ DAY 58

## טוֹב־מְעַט בִּצְדָקָה

| | |
|---|---|
| טוֹב־ | *better* |
| מְעַט | *little* |
| בִּצְדָקָה | *with righteousness/truthfulness/justice* |

## מֵרֹב תְּבוּאוֹת בְּלֹא מִשְׁפָּט:

| | |
|---|---|
| מֵרֹב תְּבוּאוֹת | *than abundance/multitude/greatness of yields/incomes* |
| בְּלֹא מִשְׁפָּט | *without justice* |

---

One who heeds a precept protects himself;
he who despises his paths will perish.

PROV 19:16 ▪ DAY 59

# עָשִׁיר בְּרָשִׁים יִמְשׁוֹל

עָשִׁיר    *rich person*

בְּרָשִׁים    *over poor people*
בְּ prep + רוֹשׁ Qal Ptcp mp

יִמְשׁוֹל    *(he) rules*
מָשַׁל Qal Impf 3ms

# וְעֶבֶד לֹוֶה לְאִישׁ מַלְוֶה:

וְעֶבֶד    *and slave/servant*

לֹוֶה    *one who borrows*
לוה Qal Ptcp ms

לְאִישׁ    *to man/person*

מַלְוֶה    *(one) who lends*
לוה Hiph Ptcp ms

A corrupt man will accept a bribe from the pocket
to divert the paths of justice.

PROV 17:23 ▪ DAY 60

כֵּן־צְדָקָה לְחַיֶּים

כֵּן־     *surely/indeed*

צְדָקָה     *righteousness/truthfulness/justice*

לְחַיֶּים     *to/for life*

וּמְרַדֵּף רָעָה לְמוֹתוֹ׃

וּמְרַדֵּף     *but one who pursues*

          Piel Ptcp ms רדף + conj וְ

רָעָה     *evil/harm/trouble*

לְמוֹתוֹ     *to/for his death*

---

Better limited assets acquired honestly
than an immense net worth amassed by mendacity.

PROV 16:8 ▪ DAY 61

מִתְאַוֶּה וָאַיִן נַפְשׁוֹ עָצֵל

מִתְאַוֶּה    *(one that) continually desires/longs*

       Hith Ptcp ms אוה

וָאַיִן    *but there is nothing*

נַפְשׁוֹ    *his soul/appetite/throat*

עָצֵל    *lazy/sluggish/slothful person*


וְנֶפֶשׁ חָרֻצִים תְּדֻשָּׁן:

וְנֶפֶשׁ חָרֻצִים    *but soul/appetite/throat of*
              *diligent/industrious people*

תְּדֻשָּׁן    *(it) is made fat/fattened*


An affluent man rules over the insolvent,
and one who borrows is a lender's slave.

PROV 22:7 ▪ DAY 62

אֱוִיל בַּיּוֹם יִוָּדַע כַּעְסוֹ

| | |
|---|---|
| אֱוִיל | *fool* |
| בַּיּוֹם | *in the day* |
| יִוָּדַע | *(it) is known* |
| | Niph Impf 3ms ידע |
| כַּעְסוֹ | *his vexation/anger/provocation* |

וְכֹסֶה קָלוֹן עָרוּם:

| | |
|---|---|
| וְכֹסֶה | *but (one who) conceals/covers* |
| | Qal Ptcp ms כסה + conj וְ |
| קָלוֹן | *shame/dishonor/disgrace* |
| עָרוּם | *prudent/shrewd/clever person* |

---

Integrity indubitably leads to life,
but pursuing depravity, to death.

PROV 11:19 ▪ DAY 63

כָּל־דַּרְכֵי־אִישׁ זַ֣ךְ בְּעֵינָ֑יו

| כָּל־דַּרְכֵי־אִישׁ | *all ways/paths of man/person* |
|---|---|
| זַ֣ךְ | *pure* |
| בְּעֵינָ֑יו | *in his eyes* |

וְתֹכֵ֖ן רוּחֹ֣ות יְהוָֽה׃

| וְתֹכֵ֖ן | *but (one who) weighs/measures/assesses* |
|---|---|
|  | Qal Ptcp ms תכן + conj וְ |
| רוּחֹ֣ות | *spirits* |
| יְהוָֽה | *YHWH* |

---

The appetite of an indolent man craves continually but has naught,
whereas the soul of the assiduous is made meaty.

PROV 13:4 ▪ DAY 64

# רַבּוֹת מַחֲשָׁבוֹת בְּלֶב־אֶישׁ

רַבּוֹת        *many*

מַחֲשָׁבוֹת    *thoughts/plans*

בְּלֶב־אֶישׁ   *in heart/mind of*
             *man/person*

# וַעֲצַת יְהוָה הִיא תָקוּם:

וַעֲצַת יְהוָה    *but counsel/plan/purpose/decision of*
               **YHWH**

הִיא           *it/that*

תָקוּם          *(it) will stand/endure/prevail*
               Qal Impf 3fs קוּם

---

An agitator's anger is made manifest during the day,
but a shrewd man hides humiliation.

PROV 12:16 ▪ DAY 65

תּוֹעֲבַת יְהוָה עִקְּשֵׁי־לֵב

| | |
|---|---|
| תּוֹעֲבַת יְהוָה | *abomination of* **YHWH** |
| עִקְּשֵׁי־לֵב | *ones crooked/twisted/perverse of heart/mind* |

וּרְצוֹנוֹ תְּמִימֵי דָרֶךְ׃

| | |
|---|---|
| וּרְצוֹנוֹ | *but his favor/delight/desire* |
| תְּמִימֵי דָרֶךְ | *ones blameless of way/path* |

---

All a man's paths are pure per his perception,
but it's YHWH who weighs spirits.

PROV 16:2 ▪ DAY 66

מִפְּרִי פִי־אִישׁ יִשְׂבַּע־טֽוֹב

| | |
|---|---|
| מִפְּרִי פִי־אִישׁ | *from fruit of*<br>*mouth of*<br>*man/person* |
| יִשְׂבַּע־ | *he is satisfied/satiated/full*<br>Qal Impf 3ms שׂבע |
| טֽוֹב | *good/goodness/benefit/well* |

וּגְמוּל יְדֵי־אָדָם יָשִׁיב לֽוֹ׃

| | |
|---|---|
| וּגְמוּל יְדֵי־אָדָם | *and dealing/deed of*<br>*hands of*<br>*man/person* |
| יָשִׁיב | *he/it will bring back*<br>Hiph Impf 3ms שׁוב<br>KETIV ישׁוב |
| לֽוֹ | *to him/himself* |

---

Many are the machinations in a man's mind,
but it's YHWH's purpose that prevails.

PROV 19:21 ▪ DAY 67

# לֵב חָכָם יַשְׂכִּיל פִּיהוּ

| | |
|---|---|
| לֵב חָכָם | *heart/mind of wise/sage person* |
| יַשְׂכִּיל | *(it) makes wise/successful // (it) teaches* <br> Hiph Impf 3ms שׂכל |
| פִּיהוּ | *his mouth* |

# וְעַל־שְׂפָתָיו יֹסִיף לֶקַח:

| | |
|---|---|
| וְעַל־שְׂפָתָיו | *and on/to his lips* |
| יֹסִיף | *it increases/adds* <br> Hiph Impf 3ms יסף |
| לֶקַח | *learning/teaching* |

---

Ones with warped minds are an abomination to YHWH,
but his favor is on those whose course is commendable.

PROV 11:20 ▪ DAY 68

זֶ֣בַח רְ֭שָׁעִים תּוֹעֲבַ֣ת יְהוָ֑ה

זֶ֣בַח רְ֭שָׁעִים   *sacrifice of*
*wicked/guilty people*

תּוֹעֲבַ֣ת יְהוָ֑ה   *abomination of*
**YHWH**

וּתְפִלַּ֖ת יְשָׁרִ֣ים רְצוֹנֽוֹ׃

וּתְפִלַּ֖ת יְשָׁרִ֣ים   *but prayer of*
*upright people*

רְצוֹנֽוֹ   *his delight/desire*

A man is well satisfied by his mouth's fruit,
and the deed of a person's hands will rebound to him.

PROV 12:14 ▪ DAY 69

טֹוב יָפִיק רָצֹון מֵיְהוָה

| | |
|---|---|
| טֹוב | *good person* |
| יָפִיק | *(he) obtains/gains/attains* |
| | Hiph Impf 3ms פוק |
| רָצֹון | *favor* |
| מֵיְהוָה | *from* YHWH |

וְאִישׁ מְזִמֹּות יַרְשִׁיעַ׃

| | |
|---|---|
| וְאִישׁ מְזִמֹּות | *but man/person of schemes/plots* |
| יַרְשִׁיעַ | *he condemns/declares guilty* |
| | Hiph Impf 3ms רשע |

> A smart man's mind gives his mouth success,
> and it adds learning to his lips.
>
> PROV 16:23 ▪ DAY 70

# בְּרָכוֹת לְרֹאשׁ צַדִּיק

בְּרָכוֹת        *blessings*

לְרֹאשׁ צַדִּיק        *for head of*
                 *righteous person*


# וּפִי רְשָׁעִים יְכַסֶּה חָמָס:

וּפִי רְשָׁעִים        *but mouth of*
                *wicked people*

יְכַסֶּה        *(it) conceals/covers up*

                Piel Impf 3ms כסה

חָמָס        *violence*


The sacrifice of the depraved is reprehensible to YHWH,
but the prayer of the upright is his delight.

PROV 15:8 • DAY 71

אִוֶּ֣לֶת שִׂמְחָ֣ה לַחֲסַר־לֵ֑ב

| | |
|---|---|
| אִוֶּ֣לֶת | *folly* |
| שִׂמְחָ֣ה | *joy/gladness/happiness/pleasure/mirth* |
| לַחֲסַר־לֵ֑ב | *to one lacking/devoid of heart/mind/understanding/ conscience* |

וְאִ֥ישׁ תְּבוּנָ֗ה יְיַשֶּׁר־לָֽכֶת׃

| | |
|---|---|
| וְאִ֥ישׁ תְּבוּנָ֗ה | *but man/person of understanding* |
| יְיַשֶּׁר־ | *(he) goes straight/makes straight* <br> Piel Impf 3ms יָשׁר |
| לָֽכֶת | *going/walking* <br> Qal Inf Cst הלך |

---

An honorable man obtains approbation from YHWH,
but a scheming man he condemns.

PROV 12:2 ▪ DAY 72

# אִישׁ חָמָס יְפַתֶּה רֵעֵהוּ

| | |
|---:|:---|
| אִישׁ חָמָס | *man/person of violence* |
| יְפַתֶּה | *(he) entices* |
| | פתה Piel Impf 3ms |
| רֵעֵהוּ | *his neighbor/friend/companion* |

# וְהוֹלִיכוֹ בְּדֶרֶךְ לֹא־טוֹב׃

| | |
|---:|:---|
| וְהוֹלִיכוֹ | *and/then he leads him* |
| | Hiph weqatal 3ms הלך + 3ms sx |
| בְּדֶרֶךְ | *in way/path* |
| לֹא־ | *not* |
| טוֹב | *good* |

---

Laurels for the head of an honorable man,
but the mouth of the viperous covers up violence.

PROV 10:6 ▪ DAY 73

## שִׂמְחָה לָאִישׁ בְּמַעֲנֵה־פִיו

| | |
|---:|---|
| שִׂמְחָה | *joy/gladness/happiness/pleasure/mirth* |
| לָאִישׁ | *to the man/person* |
| בְּמַעֲנֵה־פִיו | *in answer of his mouth* |

## וְדָבָר בְּעִתּוֹ מַה־טּוֹב:

| | |
|---:|---|
| וְדָבָר | *and word* |
| בְּעִתּוֹ | *at/in its time* |
| מַה־ | *how* |
| טּוֹב | *good/beneficial/pleasant* |

---

Folly is a joy to one deficient in sense,
but a judicious man walks straight ahead.

PROV 15:21 ▪ DAY 74

# תּוֹעֲבַת יֶהוָה שִׂפְתֵי־שָׁקֶר

תּוֹעֲבַת יֶהוָה　*abomination of*
　　　　　　　　　**YHWH**

שִׂפְתֵי־שָׁקֶר　*lips of*
　　　　　　　　　*falsehood/deceit/untruth/fraudulence*

# וְעֹשֵׂי אֱמוּנָה רְצוֹנוֹ:

וְעֹשֵׂי　*but ones who do/practice*
　　　　　Qal Ptcp mp עשׂה + conj וְ

אֱמוּנָה　*faithfulness/honesty*

רְצוֹנוֹ　*his delight/desire*

---

An injurious person entices his companion
and leads him down an inauspicious path.

PROV 16:29 ▪ DAY 75

## עִקֶּשׁ־לֵב לֹא יִמְצָא־טוֹב

עִקֶּשׁ־לֵב     *one perverse/crooked/twisted of heart/mind*

לֹא יִמְצָא־     *(he) will not find/discover/gain/obtain*
Qal Impf 3ms מצא

טוֹב     *good/goodness/benefit*


## וְנֶהְפָּךְ בִּלְשׁוֹנוֹ יִפּוֹל בְּרָעָה:

וְנֶהְפָּךְ     *and one who is perverted/twisted*
Niph Ptcp ms הפך + conj וְ

בִּלְשׁוֹנוֹ     *in/with his tongue*

יִפּוֹל     *(he) will fall*
Qal Impf 3ms נפל

בְּרָעָה     *into harm/trouble/calamity/disaster*


A man finds mirth in his mouth's answer;
indeed, how salutary is a timely word!

PROV 15:23 ▪ DAY 76

חֲכַם־לֵב יִקַּח מִצְוֺת

| | |
|---|---|
| חֲכַם־לֵב | *one wise/sage of heart/mind* |
| יִקַּח | *(he) accepts/receives*<br>Qal Impf 3ms לקח |
| מִצְוֺת | *commands/commandments/precepts* |

וֶאֱוִיל שְׂפָתַיִם יִלָּבֵט׃

| | |
|---|---|
| וֶאֱוִיל שְׂפָתַיִם | *but one foolish of lips* |
| יִלָּבֵט | *(he) will be ruined/thrust down*<br>Niph Impf 3ms לבט |

---

Malicious lips are abhorrent to YHWH,
but his delight lies with those who practice probity.

PROV 12:22 ▪ DAY 77

## בְּשִׂפְתֵי נָבוֹן תִּמָּצֵא חָכְמָה

בְּשִׂפְתֵי נָבוֹן    *on lips of*
         *one who is understanding/discerning/*
         *perceptive/intelligent*

         Niph Ptcp ms בין

תִּמָּצֵא    *(it) is found*

         Niph Impf 3fs מצא

חָכְמָה    *wisdom*

## וְשֵׁבֶט לְגֵו חֲסַר־לֵב:

וְשֵׁבֶט    *but rod*

לְגֵו חֲסַר־לֵב    *for back of*
         *one lacking/devoid of*
         *heart/mind/understanding/*
         *conscience*

---

One whose mind is warped won't obtain merit,
and he who has a forked tongue will fall into trouble.

PROV 17:20 ▪ DAY 78

פְּעֻלַּת צַדִּיק לְחַיִּים

| | |
|---|---|
| פְּעֻלַּת צַדִּיק | *wage/deed of righteous person* |
| לְחַיִּים | *to/for life* |

תְּבוּאַת רָשָׁע לְחַטָּאת:

| | |
|---|---|
| תְּבוּאַת רָשָׁע | *income/yield/produce of wicked person* |
| לְחַטָּאת | *to/for sin* |

---

He whose heart is conscientious accepts precepts,
but a man of insubordinate lips will be propelled downward.

PROV 10:8 ▪ DAY 79

כֹּפֶר לַצַּדִּיק רָשָׁע

| | |
|---|---|
| כֹּפֶר | *ransom* |
| לַצַּדִּיק | *for the righteous person* |
| רָשָׁע | *wicked/guilty person* |

וְתַחַת יְשָׁרִים בּוֹגֵד׃

| | |
|---|---|
| וְתַחַת יְשָׁרִים | *and in place of upright people* |
| בּוֹגֵד | *one who is treacherous* |
| | Qal Ptcp ms בגד |

---

Wisdom is found on an enlightened man's lips,
and the rod is for an amoral man's rear.

PROV 10:13 ▪ DAY 80

## לִפְנֵי־שֶׁבֶר יִגְבַּהּ לֵב־אִישׁ

לִפְנֵי־שֶׁבֶר     *before destruction/break/fracture/crash*

יִגְבַּהּ     *(it) is haughty/high*
          גבה Qal Impf 3ms

לֵב־אִישׁ     *heart/mind of*
          *man/person*

## וְלִפְנֵי כָבוֹד עֲנָוָה:

וְלִפְנֵי כָבוֹד     *but before honor/respect/reputation/*
          *glory*

עֲנָוָה     *humility/meekness*

---

An honest man's wage leads to life;
a wicked man's income, to impiety.

PROV 10:16  •  DAY 81

מָצָא אִשָּׁה מָצָא טוֹב

| | |
|---|---|
| מָצָא | *he found/discovered/gained/obtained* |
| | Qal Pf 3ms מצא |
| אִשָּׁה | *woman/wife* |
| מָצָא | *he found/discovered/gained/obtained* |
| | Qal Pf 3ms מצא |
| טוֹב | *good/goodness/benefit* |

וַיָּפֶק רָצוֹן מֵיהוָה:

| | |
|---|---|
| וַיָּפֶק | *since/then he obtained/gained/attained* |
| | Hiph wayyiqtol 3ms פוק |
| רָצוֹן | *favor* |
| מֵיהוָה | *from* YHWH |

---

A criminal is a ransom for a righteous man,
and a perfidious man for the upright.

PROV 21:18 ▪ DAY 82

# אֹזֶן שֹׁמַעַת וְעַיִן רֹאָה

| | |
|---|---|
| אֹזֶן | *ear* |
| שֹׁמַעַת | *(one) that hears/listens* |
| | Qal Ptcp fs שמע |
| וְעַיִן | *and eye* |
| רֹאָה | *(one) that sees* |
| | Qal Ptcp fs ראה |

# יְהוָֹה עָשָׂה גַם־שְׁנֵיהֶם:

| | |
|---|---|
| יְהוָֹה | **YHWH** |
| עָשָׂה | *(he) made* |
| | Qal Pf 3ms עשׂה |
| גַם־ | *alike* |
| שְׁנֵיהֶם | *the two of them* |

---

A man's mind is puffed up before a downfall,
but meekness precedes honor.

PROV 18:12 ▪ DAY 83

צַדִּיק מִצָּרָה נֶחֱלָץ

| | |
|---|---|
| צַדִּיק | *righteous person* |
| מִצָּרָה | *from trouble/distress* |
| נֶחֱלָץ | *(he) was delivered/rescued* |
| | Niph Pf 3ms חלץ |

וַיָּבֹא רָשָׁע תַּחְתָּיו:

| | |
|---|---|
| וַיָּבֹא | *then (he) came* |
| | Qal wayyiqtol 3ms בוא |
| רָשָׁע | *wicked/guilty person* |
| תַּחְתָּיו | *in his place* |

---

He found a wife, he found good,
since he had obtained YHWH's favor.

PROV 18:22 ▪ DAY 84

רַבִּים יְחַלּוּ פְנֵי־נָדֶיב

| | |
|---|---|
| רַבִּים | *many* |
| יְחַלּוּ | *(they) entreat/make sick* |
| | Piel Impf 3mp חלה |
| פְנֵי־נָדֶיב | *face of* |
| | *generous person/noble* |

וְכָל־הָרֵעַ לְאִישׁ מַתָּן׃

| | |
|---|---|
| וְכָל־ | *and everyone* |
| הָרֵעַ | *the friend/companion* |
| | noun רֵעַ + article |
| | *causing trouble* |
| | Hiph Inf Abs רעע |
| לְאִישׁ מַתָּן | *to/for man/person of* |
| | *gift/present* |

---

A hearing ear, a seeing eye—
YHWH made them both.

PROV 20:12 ▪ DAY 85

טֹוב יַנְחִיל בְּנֵי־בָנִים

| טֹוב | *good person* |
|---|---|

| יַנְחִיל | *(he) gives/leaves an inheritance/ his possessions* |
|---|---|

Hiph Impf 3ms נחל

| בְּנֵי־בָנִים | *children of children* |
|---|---|

וְצָפוּן לַצַדִּיק חֵיל חֹוטֵא׃

| וְצָפוּן | *and (that which) is stored/saved up* |
|---|---|

וְ + conj צפן + Qal Pass Ptcp ms

| לַצַדִּיק | *for the righteous person* |
|---|---|

| חֵיל חֹוטֵא | *wealth/property of one who sins/offends/wrongs* |
|---|---|

Qal Ptcp ms חטא

---

A righteous man was rescued from distress,
then a wicked one took his place.

PROV 11:8 ▪ DAY 86

בְּלֵב נָבוֹן תָּנוּחַ חָכְמָה

| | |
|---|---|
| בְּלֵב נָבוֹן | *in heart/mind of* <br>     *one who is understanding/discerning/* <br>     *perceptive/intelligent* <br>     Niph Ptcp ms בין |
| תָּנוּחַ | *(it) rests* <br>     Qal Impf 3fs נוח |
| חָכְמָה | *wisdom* |

וּבְקֶרֶב כְּסִילִים תִּוָּדֵעַ׃

| | |
|---|---|
| וּבְקֶרֶב כְּסִילִים | *but in midst/inner part of* <br>     *fools/dolts/idiots* |
| תִּוָּדֵעַ | *it is made known* <br>     Niph Impf 3fs ידע |

---

Many entreat a magnanimous man,
and everyone makes nice with a gift-giver.

PROV 19:6 ▪ DAY 87

עָשִׁיר וָרָשׁ נִפְגָּשׁוּ

| | |
|---|---|
| עָשִׁיר | *rich person* |
| וָרָשׁ | *and one who is poor*<br>Qal Ptcp ms רוּשׁ + conj וְ |
| נִפְגָּשׁוּ | *(they) meet together*<br>Niph Pf 3cp פגשׁ |

עֹשֵׂה כֻלָּם יְהוָה:

| | |
|---|---|
| עֹשֵׂה | *one who makes*<br>Qal Ptcp ms עשׂה |
| כֻלָּם | *all of them* |
| יְהוָה | *YHWH* |

---

A virtuous person leaves property to his posterity,
but a sinner's resources are saved up for a saint.

PROV 13:22 • DAY 88

שִׂפְתֵי כְסִיל יָבֹאוּ בְרִיב

| | |
|---:|:---|
| שִׂפְתֵי כְסִיל | *lips of* <br> *fool/dolt/idiot* |
| יָבֹאוּ | *(they) enter* <br> Qal Impf 3mp בוא |
| בְרִיב | *into strife/dispute/quarrel/argument* |

וּפִיו לְמַהֲלֻמוֹת יִקְרָא:

| | |
|---:|:---|
| וּפִיו | *and his mouth* |
| לְמַהֲלֻמוֹת | *for blows/beatings* |
| יִקְרָא | *(it) calls out/cries out* |

---

Wisdom reposes in an erudite man's heart,
but in the presence of the stupid it must be spelled out.

PROV 14:33 ▪ DAY 89

כִּשְׂחֹוק לִכְסִיל עֲשֹׂות זִמָּה

| כִּשְׂחֹוק | *like fun/sport/laughter* |
| לִכְסִיל | *for fool/dolt/idiot* |
| עֲשֹׂות | *to do/practice/execute* |
| | Qal Inf Cst עשׂה |
| זִמָּה | *wicked scheme/evil plan/depravity* |

וְחָכְמָה לְאִישׁ תְּבוּנָה׃

| וְחָכְמָה | *but wisdom* |
| לְאִישׁ תְּבוּנָה | *for man/person of understanding/discernment* |

---

Affluent and indigent will encounter each other—
YHWH's the creator of them all.

PROV 22:2 ▪ DAY 90

# צִדְקַ֣ת תָּמִ֭ים תְּיַשֵּׁ֣ר דַּרְכּ֑וֹ

| | |
|---:|:---|
| צִדְקַ֣ת תָּמִ֭ים | *righteousness/truthfulness/justice of blameless person* |
| תְּיַשֵּׁ֣ר | *(it) makes straight/upright/level* <br> Piel Impf 3fs יׁשׁר |
| דַּרְכּ֑וֹ | *his way/path* |

# וּבְרִשְׁעָת֗וֹ יִפֹּ֥ל רָשָֽׁע׃

| | |
|---:|:---|
| וּבְרִשְׁעָת֗וֹ | *but by/through his wickedness* |
| יִפֹּ֥ל | *(he) will fall* <br> Qal Impf 3ms נׁפׁל |
| רָשָֽׁע | *wicked/guilty person* |

---

An idiot's lips enter into dispute,
and his mouth cries out for castigation.

PROV 18:6 ▪ DAY 91

גַּם אֱוִיל מַחֲרִישׁ חָכָם יֵחָשֵׁב

| | |
|---|---|
| גַּם | *even* |
| אֱוִיל | *fool* |
| מַחֲרִישׁ | *(one) who is silent/quiet // keeps silent/ quiet // holds his peace* <br> Hiph Ptcp ms חרשׁ |
| חָכָם | *wise/sage* |
| יֵחָשֵׁב | *(he) is considered/thought/reckoned* <br> Niph Impf 3ms חשׁב |

אֹטֵם שְׂפָתָיו נָבוֹן:

| | |
|---|---|
| אֹטֵם | *one who shuts* <br> Qal Ptcp ms אטם |
| שְׂפָתָיו | *his lips* |
| נָבוֹן | *one who is understanding/discerning/ perceptive/intelligent* <br> Niph Ptcp ms בין |

---

Practicing depravity is fun for a fool,
but for an intelligent person, discernment.

PROV 10:23 ▪ DAY 92

עֵד בְּלִיַּעַל יָלִיץ מִשְׁפָּט

עֵד בְּלִיַּעַל — *witness/testimony of worthlessness/wickedness*

יָלִיץ — *(he/it) mocks/scorns/scoffs at*
Hiph Impf 3ms ליץ

מִשְׁפָּט — *justice*

וּפִי רְשָׁעִים יְבַלַּע־אָוֶן:

וּפִי רְשָׁעִים — *and mouth of wicked/guilty people*

יְבַלַּע־ — *(it) reports/devours/swallows*
Piel Impf 3ms בלע

אָוֶן — *iniquity/injustice/sin/evil/trouble/misfortune*

---

A blameless man's merit makes his path straight,
but a wily one will fall by his wickedness.

PROV 11:5 ▪ DAY 93

# אֹור־צַדִּיקִים יִשְׂמָח

| | |
|---|---|
| אֹור־צַדִּיקִים | *light of righteous people* |
| יִשְׂמָח | *(it) is joyful/glad/happy // (it) shines* |
| | Qal Impf 3ms שׂמח |

# וְנֵר רְשָׁעִים יִדְעָךְ:

| | |
|---|---|
| וְנֵר רְשָׁעִים | *but lamp of wicked/guilty people* |
| יִדְעָךְ | *(it) goes out/is extinguished* |
| | Qal Impf 3ms דעך |

---

Even a dolt who keeps quiet is deemed wise,
one who shuts his trap, perceptive.

PROV 17:28 ▪ DAY 94

זֶבַח רְשָׁעִים תּוֹעֵבָה

| | |
|---|---|
| זֶבַח רְשָׁעִים | *sacrifice of wicked/guilty people* |
| תּוֹעֵבָה | *abomination* |

אַף כִּי־בְזִמָּה יְבִיאֶנּוּ׃

| | |
|---|---|
| אַף כִּי־ | *how much more* |
| בְזִמָּה | *with wicked intent/evil plan/depravity* |
| יְבִיאֶנּוּ | *he brings it* |
| | Hiph Impf 3ms(!) בוא + 3ms sx |

A worthless witness jeers at justice,
and the mandibles of the wicked masticate iniquity.

PROV 19:28 ▪ DAY 95

## לֹא־יַחְפֹּץ כְּסִיל בִּתְבוּנָ֑ה

| | |
|---|---|
| לֹא־יַחְפֹּץ | *(he) does not delight/take pleasure* |
| | Qal Impf 3ms חפץ |
| כְּסִיל | *fool/dolt/idiot* |
| בִּתְבוּנָ֑ה | *in understanding/discernment* |

## כִּי אִם־בְּהִתְגַּלּ֥וֹת לִבּֽוֹ׃

| | |
|---|---|
| כִּי אִם־ | *but rather/only* |
| בְּהִתְגַּלּ֥וֹת לִבּֽוֹ | *in revealing of his heart/mind/personality* |
| | בְּ conj + גלה Hith Inf Cst |

---

The light of the guileless is luminous;
the lamp of the guilty goes out.

PROV 13:9 ▪ DAY 96

תּוֹעֲבַת יְהוָה מַחְשְׁבוֹת רָע

| | |
|---|---|
| תּוֹעֲבַת יְהוָה | *abomination of*<br>**YHWH** |
| מַחְשְׁבוֹת רָע | *thoughts/plans of*<br>*evil/harm* |

וּטְהֹרִים אִמְרֵי־נֹעַם:

| | |
|---|---|
| וּטְהֹרִים | *but pure* |
| אִמְרֵי־נֹעַם | *words of*<br>*pleasantness/kindness/favor* |

---

The sacrifice of the sinister is an abomination,
how much more when he offers it with errant intent.

PROV 21:27 ▪ DAY 97

חֲמַת־מֶ֫לֶךְ מַלְאֲכֵי־מָ֑וֶת

| חֲמַת־מֶ֫לֶךְ | *wrath/anger/fury of king/ruler* |
| מַלְאֲכֵי־מָ֑וֶת | *messengers of death* |

וְאִ֖ישׁ חָכָ֣ם יְכַפְּרֶֽנָּה׃

| וְאִ֖ישׁ | *but man/person* |
| חָכָ֣ם | *wise/sage* |
| יְכַפְּרֶֽנָּה | *(he) will appease it* |

Piel Impf 3ms כפר + 3fs sx

---

A dolt finds no delight in enlightenment
but only in manifesting his nature.

PROV 18:2 ▪ DAY 98

כֹּפֶר נֶפֶשׁ־אִישׁ עָשְׁרוֹ

| | |
|---|---|
| כֹּפֶר נֶפֶשׁ־אִישׁ | *ransom/bribe of life/soul of man/person* |
| עָשְׁרוֹ | *his wealth* |

וְרָשׁ לֹא־שָׁמַע גְּעָרָה:

| | |
|---|---|
| וְרָשׁ | *but one who is poor* |
| | Qal Ptcp ms רושׁ + conj וְ |
| לֹא־שָׁמַע | *(he) does not hear/listen to/heed* |
| | Qal Pf 3ms שׁמע |
| גְּעָרָה | *rebuke* |

---

Malevolent machinations are an abomination to YHWH,
but pleasant statements are pristine.

PROV 15:26 ▪ DAY 99

קְצַר־אַפַּיִם יַעֲשֶׂה אִוֶּלֶת

קְצַר־אַפַּיִם     *one short of [i.e., quick to]*
                   *anger*

יַעֲשֶׂה     *(he) does/practices*
           Qal Impf 3ms עשׂה

אִוֶּלֶת     *folly*


וְאִישׁ מְזִמּוֹת יִשָּׂנֵא׃

וְאִישׁ מְזִמּוֹת     *and man/person of*
                    *schemes/plots*

יִשָּׂנֵא     *(he) is hated*
            Niph Impf 3ms שׂנא


A ruler's wrath is a lethal messenger,
but a wise man can appease it.

PROV 16:14 ▪ DAY 100

טֽוֹב־עַ֭יִן ה֣וּא יְבֹרָ֑ךְ

| | |
|---|---|
| טֽוֹב־עַ֭יִן | *one good of eye* |
| ה֣וּא | *he/that one* |
| יְבֹרָ֑ךְ | *(he) will be blessed* |
| | Pual Impf 3ms ברך |

כִּֽי־נָתַ֖ן מִלַּחְמ֣וֹ לַדָּֽל׃

| | |
|---|---|
| כִּֽי־ | *for/because* |
| נָתַ֖ן | *he gives* |
| | Qal Pf 3ms נתן |
| מִלַּחְמ֣וֹ | *from his bread/food* |
| לַדָּֽל | *to the poor/weak/needy/helpless person* |

---

A man's riches are a ransom for his life,
but a poor person doesn't hearken to rebuke.

PROV 13:8 ▪ DAY 101

כָּל אֲחֵי־רָשׁ ׀ שְׂנֵאֻהוּ אַף כִּי מְרֵעֵהוּ רָחֲקוּ מִמֶּנּוּ

| | |
|---|---|
| כָּל אֲחֵי־רָשׁ ׀ | all brothers/kinsmen/relatives of one who is poor |
| | Qal Ptcp ms רוש |
| שְׂנֵאֻהוּ | (they) hate him |
| | Qal Pf 3cp שׂנא + 3ms sx |
| אַף כִּי | how much more |
| מְרֵעֵהוּ | his friends/companions |
| רָחֲקוּ | (they) are far/distant |
| | Qal Pf 3cp רחק |
| מִמֶּנּוּ | from him |

מְרַדֵּף אֲמָרִים לוֹ־הֵמָּה:

| | |
|---|---|
| מְרַדֵּף | one who pursues |
| | Piel Ptcp ms רדף |
| אֲמָרִים | words |
| לוֹ־ | to/for him |
| | KETIV ־לֹא |
| הֵמָּה | they/those/them |

A short-fused man acts stupidly,
and a conspirator is despised.

PROV 14:17 ▪ DAY 102

# רְצוֹן מְלָכִים שִׂפְתֵי־צֶדֶק

| רְצוֹן מְלָכִים | desire/delight/favor of kings/rulers |
|---|---|

| שִׂפְתֵי־צֶדֶק | lips of righteousness/honesty/justice |
|---|---|

# וְדֹבֵר יְשָׁרִים יֶאֱהָב:

**וְדֹבֵר** — and one who speaks

Qal Ptcp ms דבר + conj וְ

**יְשָׁרִים** — right/correct things

**יֶאֱהָב** — he loves

Qal Impf 3ms אהב

---

A benevolent man will doubtless be blessed
because he shares his bread with the bereft.

PROV 22:9 ▪ DAY 103

בְּכָל־עֶצֶב יִהְיֶה מוֹתָר

| בְּכָל־עֶצֶב | *in/with all toil/pain* |
|---|---|

| יִהְיֶה | *there is* |
|---|---|

Qal Impf 3ms היה

| מוֹתָר | *profit/gain* |
|---|---|

וּדְבַר־שְׂפָתַיִם אַךְ־לְמַחְסוֹר:

| וּדְבַר־שְׂפָתַיִם | *but word/speech of lips* |
|---|---|

| אַךְ־ | *surely/indeed/only* |
|---|---|

| לְמַחְסוֹר | *to/for lack/want/deficiency/privation* |
|---|---|

---

All a destitute man's relatives despise him;
how much more are his friends far from him!
One who pursues words for him—they.

PROV 19:7 ▪ DAY 104

## אֶבֶן וָאֶבֶן אֵיפָה וְאֵיפָה

| | |
|---:|:---|
| אֶבֶן | *stone/weight* |
| וָאֶבֶן | *and stone/weight* |
| אֵיפָה | *ephah/measure* |
| וְאֵיפָה | *and ephah/measure* |

## תּוֹעֲבַת יְהוָה גַּם־שְׁנֵיהֶם:

| | |
|---:|:---|
| תּוֹעֲבַת יְהוָה | *abomination of* **YHWH** |
| גַּם־ | *alike* |
| שְׁנֵיהֶם | *the two of them* |

---

Truthful lips are the delight of a potentate,
and he prizes one who speaks precisely.

PROV 16:13 ▪ DAY 105

מֶ֫לֶךְ יוֹשֵׁב עַל־כִּסֵּא־דִין

| מֶ֫לֶךְ | *king/ruler* |
|---|---|
| יוֹשֵׁב | *(one) who sits* |

          Qal Ptcp ms יֹשֵׁב

| עַל־כִּסֵּא־דִין | *on throne of*<br>*judgment* |
|---|---|

מְזָרֶה בְעֵינָיו כָּל־רָע׃

| מְזָרֶה | *(one who) scatters/winnows/discerns* |
|---|---|

          Piel Ptcp ms זרה

| בְעֵינָיו | *with his eyes* |
|---|---|
| כָּל־רָע | *all evil* |

---

There's profit in all toil,
but prattle results only in privation.

PROV 14:23 ▪ DAY 106

לֵב שָׂמֵחַ יֵיטִב פָּנִים

| | |
|---|---|
| לֵב | *heart/mind* |
| שָׂמֵחַ | *joyful/glad/happy* |
| יֵיטִב | *(it) makes good/does good to* |
| | Hiph Impf 3ms יטב |
| פָּנִים | *face* |

וּבְעַצְּבַת־לֵב רוּחַ נְכֵאָה:

| | |
|---|---|
| וּבְעַצְּבַת־לֵב | *but in/through pain/suffering/sorrow of heart/mind* |
| רוּחַ | *spirit* |
| נְכֵאָה | *broken/crushed* |

Faulty weights, misleading measures—
both are loathsome to YHWH.

PROV 20:10 ▪ DAY 107

## לֹא־יִכּוֹן אָדָם בְּרֶשַׁע

לֹא־יִכּוֹן    *(he) will not be established/secure*

Niph Impf 3ms כון

אָדָם    *man/person*

בְּרֶשַׁע    *in/by wickedness*


## וְשֹׁרֶשׁ צַדִּיקִים בַּל־יִמּוֹט:

וְשֹׁרֶשׁ צַדִּיקִים    *but root of*
                              *righteous people*

בַּל־יִמּוֹט    *(it) will not be moved/shaken*

Niph Impf 3ms מוט

---

A sovereign who sits on the dais of decision
discerns all evil with his eyes.

PROV 20:8 ▪ DAY 108

## בְּרֹב דְּבָרִים לֹא יֶחְדַּל־פָּשַׁע

| | |
|---|---|
| בְּרֹב דְּבָרִים | *in abundance/multitude of words* |
| לֹא יֶחְדַּל־ | *(it) does not cease* |
| | Qal Impf 3ms חדל |
| פָּשַׁע | *transgression/offense* |

## וְחֹשֵׂךְ שְׂפָתָיו מַשְׂכִּיל׃

| | |
|---|---|
| וְחֹשֵׂךְ | *but one who restrains* |
| | Qal Ptcp ms חשׂך + conj וְ |
| שְׂפָתָיו | *his lips* |
| מַשְׂכִּיל | *one who acts prudently/wisely/with understanding* |
| | Hiph Ptcp ms שׂכל |

---

A happy heart does the face good;
but when the heart hurts, the spirit is crushed.

PROV 15:13 ▪ DAY 109

בִּקֶּשׁ־לֵ֥ץ חָכְמָ֖ה וָאָ֑יִן

בִּקֶּשׁ־    *(he) seeks*
Piel Pf 3ms בקשׁ

לֵ֥ץ    *scoffer/scorner/mocker*

חָכְמָ֖ה    *wisdom*

וָאָ֑יִן    *but there is none*

וְדַ֖עַת לְנָב֣וֹן נָקָֽל׃

וְדַ֖עַת    *but knowledge*

לְנָב֣וֹן    *for one who is understanding/ discerning/perceptive/intelligent*
Niph Ptcp ms בין + prep לְ

נָקָֽל    *(it) is easy/swift*
Niph Pf 3ms קלל

---

A person can't be established by corruption,
but the root of the righteous won't be displaced.

PROV 12:3 ▪ DAY 110

אִישׁ מַחְסוֹר אֹהֵב שִׂמְחָה

| | |
|---|---|
| אִישׁ מַחְסוֹר | *man/person of*<br>*lack/want/deficiency/privation* |
| אֹהֵב | *one who loves*<br>אהב Qal Ptcp ms |
| שִׂמְחָה | *pleasure/mirth* |

אֹהֵב יַיִן־וָשֶׁמֶן לֹא יַעֲשִׁיר׃

| | |
|---|---|
| אֹהֵב | *one who loves*<br>אהב Qal Ptcp ms |
| ־יַיִן | *wine* |
| וָשֶׁמֶן | *and oil* |
| לֹא יַעֲשִׁיר | *(he) will not be/become rich*<br>עשר Hiph Impf 3ms |

---

Depravity is unceasing when there's a profusion of speech,
but he who shuts his trap acts shrewdly.

PROV 10:19 ▪ DAY 111

# בִּרְכַּת יְהוָה הִיא תַעֲשִׁיר

| | |
|---|---|
| בִּרְכַּת יְהוָה | *blessing of*<br>**YHWH** |
| הִיא | *it/that* |
| תַעֲשִׁיר | *(it) makes rich*<br>עשר Hiph Impf 3fs |

# וְלֹא־יוֹסִף עֶצֶב עִמָּהּ:

| | |
|---|---|
| וְלֹא־יוֹסִף | *and (he/it) does not add/increase*<br>יסף Hiph Impf 3ms |
| עֶצֶב | *toil/pain* |
| עִמָּהּ | *to/with it* |

---

A scorner seeks knowledge but there's none;
however, enlightenment comes easy to an intelligent man.

PROV 14:6 ▪ DAY 112

טֹוב אֶרֶךְ אַפַּיִם מִגִּבֹּור

| טֹוב | *better* |
|---|---|
| אֶרֶךְ אַפַּיִם | *one long of [i.e., slow to] anger* |
| מִגִּבֹּור | *than mighty person/warrior* |

וּמֹשֵׁל בְּרוּחֹו מִלֹּכֵד עִיר׃

| וּמֹשֵׁל | *and one who rules* |
|---|---|
| | וְ conj + מֹשֵׁל Qal Ptcp ms |
| בְּרוּחֹו | *over his spirit* |
| מִלֹּכֵד | *than one who captures* |
| | מִן prep + לֹכֵד Qal Ptcp ms |
| עִיר | *city* |

A lover of mirth is a person who lacks;
one enamored of wine and oil won't be wealthy.

PROV 21:17 • DAY 113

מַלְוֵה יְהוָה חוֹנֵן דָּל

מַלְוֵה    *one who lends to*
> Hiph Ptcp ms לוה

יְהוָה    **YHWH**

חוֹנֵן    *one who is gracious to/shows mercy to/ takes pity on*
> Qal Ptcp ms חנן

דָּל    *poor/weak/needy/helpless person*

וּגְמֻלוֹ יְשַׁלֶּם־לוֹ:

וּגְמֻלוֹ    *and his dealing/deed*

יְשַׁלֶּם־    *he will repay/reward/requite*
> Piel Impf 3ms שלם

לוֹ    *to him*

---

YHWH's blessing—that's what makes you rich;
and toil doesn't add to it.

PROV 10:22 ▪ DAY 114

קֹרֵץ עַיִן יִתֵּן עַצָּבֶת

קֹרֵץ     *one who winks*

    Qal Ptcp ms קרץ

עַיִן     *eye*

יִתֵּן     *(he) gives/produces*

    Qal Impf 3ms נתן

עַצָּבֶת     *pain/suffering/sorrow*

וֶאֱוִיל שְׂפָתַיִם יִלָּבֵט:

וֶאֱוִיל שְׂפָתַיִם     *and one foolish of
lips*

יִלָּבֵט     *(he) will be ruined/thrust down*

    Niph Impf 3ms לבט

---

Better a mild man than a militant,
one who rules over his spirit than one who ransacks a city.

PROV 16:32 ▪ DAY 115

לֹא יֶאֱהַב־לֵץ הוֹכֵחַ לֹו

לֹא יֶאֱהַב־   *(he) does not like/love*
Qal Impf 3ms אהב

לֵץ   *scoffer/scorner/mocker*

הוֹכֵחַ   *reproving/rebuking/refuting*
Hiph Inf Abs יכח

לֹו   *(for) him*

אֶל־חֲכָמִים לֹא יֵלֵךְ׃

אֶל־חֲכָמִים   *to/toward wise/sage people*

לֹא יֵלֵךְ   *he does not go*
Qal Impf 3ms הלך

---

One who has pity on a helpless person gives YHWH a loan,
and he'll repay him for his deed.

PROV 19:17 ▪ DAY 116

# חֲדַל־בְּנִי לִשְׁמֹעַ מוּסָר

| חֲדַל־ | *cease* |
| --- | --- |
| | Qal Impv ms חדל |

| בְּנִי | *my son/child* |
| --- | --- |

| לִשְׁמֹעַ | *to hear/listen to/heed* |
| --- | --- |
| | Qal Inf Cst שׁמע + prep לְ |

| מוּסָר | *instruction/training/education/warning/ discipline/correction/chastisement* |
| --- | --- |

# לִשְׁגוֹת מֵאִמְרֵי־דָעַת:

| לִשְׁגוֹת | *to stray* |
| --- | --- |
| | Qal Inf Cst שׁגה + prep לְ |

| מֵאִמְרֵי־דָעַת | *from words of knowledge* |
| --- | --- |

---

A conniver produces pain,
and a rash-lipped man will be ruined.

PROV 10:10 ▪ DAY 117

בְּכָל־עֵת אֹהֵב הָרֵעַ

| | |
|---|---|
| בְּכָל־עֵת | *in/at every time* |
| אֹהֵב | *(one who) likes/loves* |
| | Qal Ptcp ms אהב |
| הָרֵעַ | *the friend/companion* |
| | noun רֵעַ + article |
| | *causing trouble* |
| | Hiph Inf Abs רעע |

וְאָח לְצָרָה יִוָּלֵד:

| | |
|---|---|
| וְאָח | *but/and brother/kinsman/relative* |
| לְצָרָה | *for trouble/distress* |
| יִוָּלֵד | *(he) is born* |
| | Niph Impf 3ms ילד |

---

A scoffer doesn't appreciate being reproofed;
he won't approach the wise.

PROV 15:12 ▪ DAY 118

אֹזֶן שֹׁמַעַת תּוֹכַחַת חַיִּים

| | |
|---|---|
| אֹזֶן | *ear* |
| שֹׁמַעַת | *(one) that hears/listens to/heeds* |
| | Qal Ptcp fs שמע |
| תּוֹכַחַת חַיִּים | *reproof/rebuke of* *life* |

בְּקֶרֶב חֲכָמִים תָּלִין:

| | |
|---|---|
| בְּקֶרֶב חֲכָמִים | *in midst/inner part of* *wise/sage people* |
| תָּלִין | *it lodges/stays/remains* |
| | Qal Impf 3fs לין |

Stop heeding instruction, my son,
so as to stray from words of knowledge.

PROV 19:27 ▪ DAY 119

אֶרֶךְ אַפַּיִם רַב־תְּבוּנָה

אֶרֶךְ אַפַּיִם    *one long of [i.e., slow to]*
*anger*

רַב־תְּבוּנָה    *one great/abundant of*
*understanding/discernment*

וּקְצַר־רֹוּחַ מֵרִים אִוֶּלֶת:

וּקְצַר־רֹוּחַ    *and one short [i.e., quick] of*
*spirit [i.e., temper]*

מֵרִים    *one who exalts*

Hiph Ptcp ms רום

אִוֶּלֶת    *folly*

---

An acquaintance is affable all the time,
but a brother is born for trouble.

PROV 17:17 ▪ DAY 120

צְדָקָה תִּצֹּר תָּם־דָּרֶךְ

| | |
|---|---|
| צְדָקָה | *righteousness/truthfulness/justice* |
| תִּצֹּר | *(it) guards/protects/preserves* |
| תָּם־דָּרֶךְ | *integrity/innocence/blamelessness/ purity/perfection of way* |

וְרִשְׁעָה תְּסַלֵּף חַטָּאת:

| | |
|---|---|
| וְרִשְׁעָה | *but wickedness* |
| תְּסַלֵּף | *(it) overthrows/ruins/subverts* Piel Impf 3fs סלף |
| חַטָּאת | *sin/sinner* |

An ear that listens to a life-giving rebuke—
it makes its home among the comprehending.

PROV 15:31 ▪ DAY 121

חוֹשֵׂךְ שִׁבְטוֹ שׂוֹנֵא בְנוֹ

חוֹשֵׂךְ    *one who restrains/withholds/holds back*
           Qal Ptcp ms חשׂך

שִׁבְטוֹ    *his rod*

שׂוֹנֵא    *one who hates*
           Qal Ptcp ms שׂנא

בְנוֹ    *his son/child*

וְאֹהֲבוֹ שִׁחֲרוֹ מוּסָר:

וְאֹהֲבוֹ    *but one who loves him*
           Qal Ptcp ms אהב + 3ms sx + conj וְ

שִׁחֲרוֹ    *(he) earnestly/diligently seeks him*
           Piel Pf 3ms שׁחר + 3ms sx

מוּסָר    *discipline/correction/chastisement/*
               *warning/instruction/training/education*

---

A serene man has a great deal of discernment,
but a hothead trots out drivel.

PROV 14:29 • DAY 122

# מוּסָר רָע לְעֹזֵב אֹרַח

| מוּסָר | *discipline/correction/chastisement/ warning/instruction/training/education* |
| רָע | *severe/difficult/calamitous* |
| לְעֹזֵב | *for one who abandons/forsakes* |
| | Qal Ptcp ms עזב + prep לְ |
| אֹרַח | *way/path* |

# שׂוֹנֵא תוֹכַחַת יָמוּת:

| שׂוֹנֵא | *one who hates* |
| | Qal Ptcp ms שׂנא |
| תוֹכַחַת | *reproof/rebuke* |
| יָמוּת | *(he) will die* |
| | Qal Impf 3ms מות |

Righteousness preserves one whose way is scrupulous,
but depravity subverts a sinner.

PROV 13:6 ▪ DAY 123

## עֲטֶרֶת תִּפְאֶרֶת שֵׂיבָה

עֲטֶרֶת תִּפְאֶרֶת      *crown of*
                    *glory/splendor/honor/beauty*

שֵׂיבָה      *old age/gray hair*

## בְּדֶרֶךְ צְדָקָה תִּמָּצֵא:

בְּדֶרֶךְ צְדָקָה      *in/on/through way/path of*
                   *righteousness/truthfulness/justice*

תִּמָּצֵא      *it is found/gained/obtained/reached*
             Niph Impf 3fs מצא

---

He who withholds his rod hates his son,
but he who loves him will diligently desire to discipline him.

PROV 13:24 ▪ DAY 124

# אִישׁ תַּהְפֻּכוֹת יְשַׁלַּח מָדְוֹן

| | |
|---|---|
| אִישׁ תַּהְפֻּכוֹת | *man of perversities* |
| יְשַׁלַּח | *(he) sends forth/lets loose* <br> Piel Impf 3ms שׁלח |
| מָדְוֹן | *strife/contention* |

# וְנִרְגָּן מַפְרִיד אַלּוּף׃

| | |
|---|---|
| וְנִרְגָּן | *and one who gossips/whispers/slanders* <br> Niph Ptcp ms רגן + conj וְ |
| מַפְרִיד | *one who separates* <br> Hiph Ptcp ms פרד |
| אַלּוּף | *close friend* |

---

Draconian discipline for him who deviates from the path;
he who detests censure will die.

PROV 15:10 ▪ DAY 125

## אֹרַח לְחַיִּים שׁוֹמֵר מוּסָר

| | |
|---|---|
| אֹרַח | *way/path* |
| לְחַיִּים | *to life* |
| שׁוֹמֵר | *one who heeds/guards/keeps* <br> Qal Ptcp ms שׁמר |
| מוּסָר | *instruction/training/education/warning/ discipline/correction/chastisement* |

## וְעוֹזֵב תּוֹכַחַת מַתְעֶה:

| | |
|---|---|
| וְעוֹזֵב | *but one who abandons/forsakes/neglects* <br> Qal Ptcp ms עזב + conj וְ |
| תּוֹכַחַת | *reproof/rebuke* |
| מַתְעֶה | *one who leads astray* <br> Hiph Ptcp ms תעה |

---

Gray hair is a beautiful tiara;
it's found on the virtuous route.

PROV 16:31 ▪ DAY 126

גּוֹלֶה־סוֹד הוֹלֵךְ רָכִיל

| גּוֹלֶה־ | one who reveals |
| | Qal Ptcp ms גלה |
| סוֹד | secret |
| הוֹלֵךְ | one who goes about with |
| | Qal Ptcp ms הלך |
| רָכִיל | slander |

וּלְפֹתֶה שְׂפָתָיו לֹא תִתְעָרָב׃

| וּלְפֹתֶה | and with one who opens // one who is inexperienced/naïve regarding |
| | Qal Ptcp ms פתה + prep לְ + conj וְ |
| שְׂפָתָיו | his lips |
| לֹא תִתְעָרָב | you should not associate |
| | Hith Impf 2ms ערב |

A perverse person lets loose strife,
and a gossiper separates good friends.

PROV 16:28 ▪ DAY 127

# עֶבֶד־מַשְׂכִּיל יִמְשֹׁל בְּבֵן מֵבִישׁ

| | |
|---|---|
| עֶבֶד־ | *servant/slave* |
| מַשְׂכִּיל | *(one) who acts prudently/wisely/with understanding*<br>Hiph Ptcp ms שׂכל |
| יִמְשֹׁל | *(he) will rule*<br>Qal Impf 3ms משׁל |
| בְּבֵן | *over son/child* |
| מֵבִישׁ | *(one) who acts shamefully/causes shame*<br>Hiph Ptcp ms בושׁ |

# וּבְתוֹךְ אַחִים יַחֲלֹק נַחֲלָה׃

| | |
|---|---|
| וּבְתוֹךְ אַחִים | *and in midst of brothers* |
| יַחֲלֹק | *he will divide/share*<br>Qal Impf 3ms חלק |
| נַחֲלָה | *inheritance/property* |

---

Heeding instruction is the path to vitality,
but one who abandons admonition leads others astray.

PROV 10:17 ▪ DAY 128

# הוֹלֵךְ רָכִיל מְגַלֶּה־סּוֹד

| הוֹלֵךְ | one who goes about with |
| --- | --- |
| | Qal Ptcp ms הלךְ |

| רָכִיל | slander |
| --- | --- |

| מְגַלֶּה־ | one who reveals |
| --- | --- |
| | Piel Ptcp ms גלה |

| סוֹד | secret |
| --- | --- |

# וְנֶאֱמַן־רוּחַ מְכַסֶּה דָבָר:

| וְנֶאֱמַן־רוּחַ | but one who is faithful/trustworthy of spirit |
| --- | --- |
| | Niph Ptcp ms אמן + conj וְ |

| מְכַסֶּה | one who conceals |
| --- | --- |
| | Piel Ptcp ms כסה |

| דָבָר | matter/word/speech |
| --- | --- |

---

A slanderer can disclose a secret,
so don't associate with someone of indiscreet lips.

PROV 20:19 ▪ DAY 129

## רָאשׁ עֹשֶׂה כַף־רְמִיָּה

רָאשׁ     *one who is poor*
         Qal Ptcp ms רושׁ

עֹשֶׂה     *one who works*
         Qal Ptcp ms עשׂה

כַף־רְמִיָּה     *hand/palm of*
         *slackness/indolence/negligence/*
         *deceit/treachery*


## וְיַד חָרוּצִים תַּעֲשִׁיר:

וְיַד חָרוּצִים     *but hand of*
         *diligent/industrious people/[golds]*

תַּעֲשִׁיר     *(it) becomes/makes rich*
         Hiph Impf 3fs עשׁר

---

A wise slave will rule over a shameful child,
and among the brothers he will share the inheritance.

PROV 17:2 ▪ DAY 130

מַרְפֵּא לָשׁוֹן עֵץ חַיִּים

| | |
|---|---|
| מַרְפֵּא לָשׁוֹן | *gentleness/calmness/healing of tongue* |
| עֵץ חַיִּים | *tree of life* |

וְסֶלֶף בָּהּ שֶׁבֶר בְּרוּחַ׃

| | |
|---|---|
| וְסֶלֶף | *but perversity/twistedness/subversion* |
| בָּהּ | *in/on it* |
| שֶׁבֶר | *destruction/break/fracture/crash* |
| בְּרוּחַ | *in spirit* |

---

A calumniator betrays a confidence,
but one whose spirit is trustworthy stays mum about a matter.

PROV 11:13 ▪ DAY 131

מַחְשְׁבוֹת חָרוּץ אַךְ־לְמוֹתָר

| | |
|---|---|
| מַחְשְׁבוֹת חָרוּץ | *plans/thoughts of diligent/industrious person/[gold]* |
| אַךְ־ | *surely/indeed/only* |
| לְמוֹתָר | *to/for profit/gain/advantage* |

וְכָל־אָץ אַךְ־לְמַחְסוֹר:

| | |
|---|---|
| וְכָל־ | *but every* |
| אָץ | *one who hurries/is hasty* <br> Qal Ptcp ms אוץ |
| אַךְ־ | *surely/indeed/only* |
| לְמַחְסוֹר | *to/for lack/want/deficiency/privation* |

---

An indigent man works with an indolent hand,
but the fist of the diligent gets rich.

PROV 10:4 ▪ DAY 132

לֵץ תַּכֶּה וּפֶתִי יַעְרִם

| | |
|---|---|
| לֵץ | scoffer/scorner/mocker |
| תַּכֶּה | you strike<br>Hiph Impf 2ms נכה |
| וּפֶתִי | and simpleminded/naïve/ignorant person |
| יַעְרִם | (he) will become prudent/shrewd<br>Hiph Impf 3ms ערם |

וְהוֹכִיחַ לְנָבוֹן יָבִין דָּעַת׃

| | |
|---|---|
| וְהוֹכִיחַ | and to reprove/rebuke<br>Hiph Inf Cst יכח + conj וְ |
| לְנָבוֹן | one who is understanding/discerning/perceptive/intelligent<br>Niph Ptcp ms בין + prep לְ |
| יָבִין | he will understand/discern/perceive<br>Qal Impf 3ms בין |
| דָּעַת | knowledge |

---

A gentle tongue is a tree of life,
but when perversity's on it, there's a rupture in spirit.

PROV 15:4 ▪ DAY 133

יֶלֵד כְּסִיל לְתוּגָה לֽוֹ

| | |
|---|---|
| יֹלֵד | one who fathers/begets |
| | Qal Ptcp ms ילד |
| כְּסִיל | fool/dolt/idiot |
| לְתוּגָה | to/for grief/sorrow |
| לֽוֹ | to/for him |

וְלֹא־יִשְׂמַח אֲבִי נָבָֽל׃

| | |
|---|---|
| וְלֹא־יִשְׂמַח | and (he) is not joyful/glad/happy |
| | Qal Impf 3ms שׂמח |
| אֲבִי נָבָל | father of foolish/ignominious/godless/ worthless person |

An industrious man's plans indubitably lead to gain,
but everyone who is hasty will surely have a shortage.

PROV 21:5 ▪ DAY 134

הֹון יְסִיף רֵעִים רַבִּים

| | |
|---|---|
| הֹון | *wealth* |
| יְסִיף | *(it) adds/increases* |
| | יסף Hiph Impf 3ms |
| רֵעִים | *friends/companions* |
| רַבִּים | *many* |

וְדָל מֵרֵעֵהוּ יִפָּרֵד:

| | |
|---|---|
| וְדָל | *but poor/weak/needy/helpless person* |
| מֵרֵעֵהוּ | *from his friend* |
| יִפָּרֵד | *(he) is separated* |
| | פרד Niph Impf 3ms |

---

If you slap a mocker, a simpleton becomes prudent,
and admonish an enlightened man, he will comprehend knowledge.

PROV 19:25 ▪ DAY 135

# צִדְקַת יְשָׁרִים תַּצִּילֵם

צִדְקַת יְשָׁרִים  *righteousness/truthfulness/justice of upright people*

תַּצִּילֵם  *(it) delivers/rescues them*

Hiph Impf 3fs נצל + 3mp sx

# וּבְהַוַּת בֹּגְדִים יִלָּכֵדוּ׃

וּבְהַוַּת בֹּגְדִים  *but by desire/greed/craving/malice of ones who are treacherous*

Qal Ptcp mp בגד

יִלָּכֵדוּ  *they are captured/caught*

Niph Impf 3mp לכד

---

When a man fathers a fool, it's to his chagrin;
indeed, the parent of a rogue isn't cheerful.

PROV 17:21 ▪ DAY 136

לֹא־יוֹעִילוּ אוֹצְרוֹת רֶ֫שַׁע

לֹא־יוֹעִילוּ　*(they) do not profit*

יָעַל Hiph Impf 3mp

אוֹצְרוֹת רֶ֫שַׁע　*treasures of*
　　　　　　　　　*wickedness*

וּצְדָקָה תַּצִּיל מִמָּוֶת:

וּצְדָקָה　*but righteousness/truthfulness/justice*

תַּצִּיל　*(it) delivers/rescues*

נָצַל Hiph Impf 3fs

מִמָּוֶת　*from death*

---

Capital adds a crowd of companions,
but a bankrupt man is separated even from his best friend.

PROV 19:4 ▪ DAY 137

# מַחֲשָׁבוֹת בְּעֵצָה תִּכּוֹן

מַחֲשָׁבוֹת    *thoughts/plans*

בְּעֵצָה    *by counsel/advice*

תִּכּוֹן    *(it) will be established/secure/ready*
     Niph Impf 3fs(!) כון

# וּבְתַחְבֻּלוֹת עֲשֵׂה מִלְחָמָה:

וּבְתַחְבֻּלוֹת    *and by counsels/guidance*

עֲשֵׂה    *make*
     Qal Impv ms עשׂה

מִלְחָמָה    *war*

---

The righteousness of the upright rescues them,
but renegades are caught by their own greed.

PROV 11:6 ▪ DAY 138

# עִיר גִּבֹּרִים עָלָה חָכָם

| | |
|---|---|
| עִיר גִּבֹּרִים | city of |
| | mighty people/warriors |
| עָלָה | (he) went up/ascended |
| | Qal Pf 3ms עלה |
| חָכָם | wise/sage person |

# וַיֹּרֶד עֹז מִבְטֶחָה׃

| | |
|---|---|
| וַיֹּרֶד | then (he) brought down |
| | Hiph wayyiqtol 3ms ירד |
| עֹז מִבְטֶחָה | strength of |
| | its confidence/trust |

---

Filthy lucre doesn't profit,
but righteousness delivers from death.

PROV 10:2 ▪ DAY 139

## רֵישׁ וְקָלוֹן פּוֹרֵעַ מוּסָר

| רֵישׁ | *poverty* |
|---|---|
| וְקָלוֹן | *and shame/dishonor/disgrace* |
| פּוֹרֵעַ | *one who ignores/avoids*<br>Qal Ptcp ms פרע |
| מוּסָר | *instruction/training/education/warning/*<br>*discipline/correction/chastisement* |

## וְשׁוֹמֵר תּוֹכַחַת יְכֻבָּד:

| וְשׁוֹמֵר | *but one who heeds/guards/keeps*<br>Qal Ptcp ms שמר + conj וְ |
|---|---|
| תּוֹכַחַת | *reproof/rebuke* |
| יְכֻבָּד | *(he) will be honored*<br>Pual Impf 3ms כבד |

---

Stratagems are established through deliberation,
so make war with guidance.

PROV 20:18 ▪ DAY 140

עֲטֶרֶת זְקֵנִים בְּנֵי בָנִים

עֲטֶרֶת זְקֵנִים    *crown of*
                *old people*

בְּנֵי בָנִים    *children of*
              *children*

וְתִפְאֶרֶת בָּנִים אֲבוֹתָם:

וְתִפְאֶרֶת בָּנִים    *and glory/splendor/honor/beauty of*
                 *children*

אֲבוֹתָם    *their fathers/parents/forebears*

---

A wise man scaled the warriors' city,
then he toppled its self-assured fortitude.

PROV 21:22 ▪ DAY 141

בָּז לְדָבָר יֵחָבֶל לוֹ

בָּז     *one who despises*
      Qal Ptcp ms בוז

לְדָבָר     *word/matter*

יֵחָבֶל     *(he) will be harmed // (he) will be held in pledge*
      Niph Impf 3ms חבל

לוֹ     *because of it // for it*


וִירֵא מִצְוָה הוּא יְשֻׁלָּם:

וִירֵא מִצְוָה     *but one fearful/reverent/respectful of command/commandment/precept*

הוּא     *he/that one*

יְשֻׁלָּם     *(he) will be rewarded/repaid/requited*
      Pual Impf 3ms שלם

---

Indigence and ignominy for one who ignores instruction,
but one who heeds rebuke will be revered.

PROV 13:18 ▪ DAY 142

הוֹן עָשִׁיר קִרְיַת עֻזּוֹ

| | |
|---|---|
| הוֹן עָשִׁיר | *wealth of rich person* |
| קִרְיַת עֻזּוֹ | *city of his strength* |

מְחִתַּת דַּלִּים רֵישָׁם:

| | |
|---|---|
| מְחִתַּת דַּלִּים | *ruin/terror of poor/weak/needy/helpless people* |
| רֵישָׁם | *their poverty* |

Descendants are the diadem of the aged,
and the grandeur of children is their ancestors.

PROV 17:6 ▪ DAY 143

בְּאֵין תַּחְבֻּלוֹת יִפָּל־עָם

| | |
|---|---|
| בְּאֵין | *when there is/are no* |
| תַּחְבֻּלוֹת | *counsels/guidance* |
| יִפָּל־ | *(it) falls* |
| | Qal Impf 3ms נפל |
| עָם | *people/nation* |

וּתְשׁוּעָה בְּרֹב יוֹעֵץ:

| | |
|---|---|
| וּתְשׁוּעָה | *but deliverance/rescue/victory* |
| בְּרֹב יוֹעֵץ | *in abundance/multitude of one who counsels/advises* |
| | Qal Ptcp ms(!) יעץ |

---

He who despises a dictum will be harmed for it,
but he who respects a precept will surely be rewarded.

PROV 13:13 ▪ DAY 144

עֵד שְׁקָרִים לֹא יִנָּקֶה

עֵד שְׁקָרִים   *witness/testimony of*
*falsehoods/deceptions/lies/untruths*

לֹא יִנָּקֶה   *(he/it) will not go unpunished*
Niph Impf 3ms נקה


וְיָפִיחַ כְּזָבִים לֹא יִמָּלֵט:

וְיָפִיחַ   *and witness of*
וְ + conj יָפִיחַ noun
*and he breathes out/pours out*
וְ + conj פוח Hiph Impf 3ms

כְּזָבִים   *lies/falsehoods*

לֹא יִמָּלֵט   *(he) will not escape*
Niph Impf 3ms מלט


A prosperous person's capital is his mighty city;
the nightmare of the helpless is their mendicancy.

PROV 10:15 • DAY 145

עֹשֵׁק דָּל לְהַרְבּוֹת לוֹ

| | |
|---:|:---|
| עֹשֵׁק | one who oppresses/exploits/defrauds/abuses |
| | Qal Ptcp ms עשק |
| דָּל | poor/weak/needy/helpless person |
| לְהַרְבּוֹת | to make increase |
| | לְ prep + רבה Hiph Inf Cst |
| לוֹ | for him/himself |

נֹתֵן לְעָשִׁיר אַךְ־לְמַחְסוֹר׃

| | |
|---:|:---|
| נֹתֵן | one who gives |
| | Qal Ptcp ms נתן |
| לְעָשִׁיר | to rich person |
| אַךְ־ | surely/indeed/only/however/yet/but |
| לְמַחְסוֹר | to/for lack/want/deficiency/privation |

---

When guidance is absent, a people falls;
but success comes through a cohort of counselors.

PROV 11:14 ▪ DAY 146

## עָרוּם| רָאָה רָעָה וְנִסְתָּר

| עָרוּם| | *prudent/shrewd/clever person* |
|---|---|
| רָאָה | *(he) saw* |
| | Qal Pf 3ms ראה |
| רָעָה | *evil/harm/trouble/calamity/disaster* |
| וְנִסְתָּר | *and/then (he) hid* |
| | Niph weqatal 3ms סתר |
| | ויסתר KETIV |

## וּפְתָיִים עָברוּ וְנֶעֱנָשׁוּ׃

| וּפְתָיִים | *but simpleminded/naïve/ignorant people* |
|---|---|
| עָבְרוּ | *(they) passed by/on* |
| | Qal Pf 3cp עבר |
| וְנֶעֱנָשׁוּ | *and/then (they) were punished* |
| | Niph weqatal 3cp ענש |

---

A perjurious witness will not go unpunished,
and one who pours out prevarications will not escape.

PROV 19:5 ▪ DAY 147

# בָּז־לְרֵעֵהוּ חוֹטֵא

| | |
|---|---|
| בָּז־ | *one who despises* |
| | Qal Ptcp ms בוז |
| לְרֵעֵהוּ | *his neighbor/friend/companion* |
| חוֹטֵא | *one who sins/offends/wrongs* |
| | Qal Ptcp ms חטא |

# וּמְחוֹנֵן עֲנָוִים אַשְׁרָיו:

| | |
|---|---|
| וּמְחוֹנֵן | *but one who is gracious to/shows mercy to/takes pity on* |
| | Polel Ptcp ms חנן + conj וְ |
| עֲנָוִים | *lowly/afflicted/humble/dejected people* |
| | KETIV עניים |
| אַשְׁרָיו | *blessed/happy is he* |

---

Oppressing a poor person to pile up proceeds for oneself,
donating to an opulent one—the only eventuality is want.

PROV 22:16 ▪ DAY 148

אֵשֶׁת־חַיִל עֲטֶרֶת בַּעְלָהּ

אֵשֶׁת־חַיִל  *wife of*
            *strength/valor/wealth/property*

עֲטֶרֶת בַּעְלָהּ  *crown of*
                *her husband*

וּכְרָקָב בְּעַצְמוֹתָיו מְבִישָׁה:

וּכְרָקָב  *but like rot/decay*

בְּעַצְמוֹתָיו  *in his bones*

מְבִישָׁה  *one who acts shamefully/causes shame*
          Hiph Ptcp fs בושׁ

A prudent person espied evil and disappeared,
but the callow continued along and were castigated.

PROV 22:3 ▪ DAY 149

לֵב צַדִּיק יֶהְגֶּה לַעֲנוֹת

לֵב צַדִּיק    *heart/mind of*
*righteous person*

יֶהְגֶּה    *(it) ponders/meditates/considers*
Qal Impf 3ms הגה

לַעֲנוֹת    *to answer/speak up*
ל prep + עשׂה Qal Inf Cst

וּפִי רְשָׁעִים יַבִּיעַ רָעוֹת:

וּפִי רְשָׁעִים    *but mouth of*
*wicked/guilty people*

יַבִּיעַ    *(it) spews/pours forth*
נבע Hiph Impf 3ms

רָעוֹת    *evils*

---

He who despises his neighbor sins,
but he who is benevolent to the shunned is blessed.

PROV 14:21 ▪ DAY 150

## הֵעֵז אִישׁ רָשָׁע בְּפָנָיו

| | |
|---|---|
| הֵעֵז | *(he) makes strong/firm/defiant* |
| | Hiph Pf 3ms עזז |
| אִישׁ | *man/person* |
| רָשָׁע | *wicked* |
| בְּפָנָיו | *his face* |

## וְיָשָׁר הוּא׀ יָבִין דַּרְכּוֹ׃

| | |
|---|---|
| וְיָשָׁר | *but upright person* |
| הוּא׀ | *he/that one* |
| יָבִין | *(he) understands/discerns/perceives* |
| | Qal Impf 3ms בין |
| | KETIV יכין |
| דַּרְכּוֹ | *his way/path* |
| | KETIV דרכיו |

---

A heroic wife is her husband's crown,
but she who causes shame is like rot in his bones.

PROV 12:4 ▪ DAY 151

מַצְדִּיק רָשָׁע וּמַרְשִׁיעַ צַדִּיק

| | |
|---|---|
| מַצְדִּיק | *one who vindicates/declares righteous* |
| | Hiph Ptcp ms צדק |
| רָשָׁע | *wicked/guilty person* |
| וּמַרְשִׁיעַ | *and one who condemns/declares wicked/declares guilty* |
| | וְ + conj Hiph Ptcp ms רשע |
| צַדִּיק | *righteous person* |

תּוֹעֲבַת יְהֹוָה גַּם־שְׁנֵיהֶם:

| | |
|---|---|
| תּוֹעֲבַת יְהֹוָה | *abomination of YHWH* |
| גַּם־ | *alike* |
| שְׁנֵיהֶם | *the two of them* |

A righteous mind thinks before replying,
but the mouth of the wicked spews smears.

PROV 15:28 ▪ DAY 152

# לֹא־יַרְעִיב יְהוָה נֶפֶשׁ צַדִּיק

לֹא־יַרְעִיב    *(he) does not let go hungry*

Hiph Impf 3ms רעב

יְהוָה    **YHWH**

נֶפֶשׁ צַדִּיק    *soul/appetite/throat of*
*righteous person*

# וְהַוַּת רְשָׁעִים יֶהְדֹּף׃

וְהַוַּת רְשָׁעִים    *but desire/greed/craving of*
*wicked people*

יֶהְדֹּף    *he shoves/pushes/thrusts away*

Qal Impf 3ms הדף

---

A depraved man renders his face defiant,
but a dignified one discerns his way.

PROV 21:29 ▪ DAY 153

שַׁחוּ רָעִים לִפְנֵי טוֹבִים

| | |
|---|---|
| שַׁחוּ | *(they) bow down/crouch* |
| שחח Qal Pf 3cp | |
| רָעִים | *evil/bad people* |
| לִפְנֵי טוֹבִים | *before good people* |

וּרְשָׁעִים עַל־שַׁעֲרֵי צַדִּיק׃

| | |
|---|---|
| וּרְשָׁעִים | *and wicked people* |
| עַל־שַׁעֲרֵי צַדִּיק | *at gates of righteous person* |

---

Granting a criminal clemency and locking up the guiltless—
both are outrageous to YHWH.

PROV 17:15 ▪ DAY 154

שִׂפְתֵי צַדִּיק יֵדְעוּן רָצוֹן

| שִׂפְתֵי צַדִּיק | *lips of* |
| | *righteous person* |

| יֵדְעוּן | *(they) know* |
| | Qal Impf 3mp ידע |

| רָצוֹן | *favor/delight* |

וּפִי רְשָׁעִים תַּהְפֻּכוֹת׃

| וּפִי רְשָׁעִים | *but mouth of* |
| | *wicked people* |

| תַּהְפֻּכוֹת | *perversities* |

---

YHWH doesn't let a scrupulous person go hungry,
but he shoves away the craving of the contemptible.

PROV 10:3 ▪ DAY 155

שְׁאוֹל וַאֲבַדּוֹן נֶגֶד יְהוָה

שְׁאוֹל   *Sheol/underworld/netherworld/grave*

וַאֲבַדּוֹן   *and Abaddon/destruction/perdition*

נֶגֶד יְהוָה   *before YHWH*

אַף כִּי־לִבּוֹת בְּנֵי־אָדָם:

אַף כִּי־   *how much more*

לִבּוֹת בְּנֵי־אָדָם   *hearts/minds/consciences of*
*children of*
*humankind/humanity*

---

The pernicious prostrate themselves before the benevolent,
and the reprehensible at the gates of a righteous one.

PROV 14:19 ▪ DAY 156

אִוֶּלֶת אָדָם תְּסַלֵּף דַּרְכּוֹ

אִוֶּלֶת אָדָם  *folly of*
man/person/humankind/humanity

תְּסַלֵּף  *(it) overthrows/ruins/subverts*
סלף Piel Impf 3fs

דַּרְכּוֹ  *his/its way*

וְעַל־יְהוָֹה יִזְעַף לִבּוֹ:

וְעַל־יְהוָֹה  *and/but against* YHWH

יִזְעַף  *(it) rages/is vexed*
זעף Qal Impf 3ms

לִבּוֹ  *his/its heart/mind*

---

A virtuous man's lips know delight,
but the mouth of the perfidious, perversities.

PROV 10:32 ▪ DAY 157

מִדְּרָכָיו יִשְׂבַּע סוּג לֵב

מִדְּרָכָיו    *from his ways*

יִשְׂבַּע    *(he) is satisfied/satiated*
     Qal Impf 3ms שׂבע

סוּג לֵב    *one who is unfaithful/backsliding/*
     *fenced in of*
       *heart/mind*
     Qal Ptcp ms סוג

וּמֵעָלָיו אִישׁ טוֹב:

וּמֵעָלָיו    *and from upon him [(!)* READ: *and his*
     *deeds]*

אִישׁ    *man/person*

טוֹב    *good*

---

The underworld and infernal realm are before YHWH,
how much more the hearts of humankind!

PROV 15:11 ▪ DAY 158

פַּלְגֵי־מַיִם לֶב־מֶלֶךְ בְּיַד־יְהוָה

| | |
|---|---|
| פַּלְגֵי־מַיִם | streams/channels of water |
| לֶב־מֶלֶךְ | heart/mind of king/ruler |
| בְּיַד־יְהוָה | in hand/power/control of **YHWH** |

עַל־כָּל־אֲשֶׁר יַחְפֹּץ יַטֶּנּוּ׃

| | |
|---|---|
| עַל־כָּל־אֲשֶׁר יַחְפֹּץ | on/toward all that he desires/delights in/takes pleasure in |
| | Qal Impf 3ms חפץ |
| יַטֶּנּוּ | he turns/inclines/diverts it |
| | Hiph Impf 3ms נטה + 3ms sx |

Humanity's hubris overthrows its course;
indeed, its heart seethes against YHWH.

PROV 19:3 ▪ DAY 159

לֵב אָדָם יְחַשֵּׁב דַּרְכֹּו

| | |
|---|---|
| לֵב אָדָם | *heart/mind of man/person/humankind/humanity* |
| יְחַשֵּׁב | *(it) considers/plans*<br>Piel Impf 3ms חשׁב |
| דַּרְכֹּו | *his/its way/path* |

וַיהוָה יָכִין צַעֲדֹו:

| | |
|---|---|
| וַיהוָה | *and/but* YHWH |
| יָכִין | *(he) prepares/determines/makes firm/ establishes/directs*<br>Hiph Impf 3ms כון |
| צַעֲדֹו | *his/its step* |

---

A soulless man is satisfied with his ways,
likewise a dignified man with his deeds.

PROV 14:14 ▪ DAY 160

רָחֹוק יְהֹוָה מֵרְשָׁעִים

| | |
|---|---|
| רָחֹוק | *far/distant* |
| יְהֹוָה | *YHWH* |
| מֵרְשָׁעִים | *from wicked people* |

וּתְפִלַּת צַדִּיקִים יִשְׁמָע׃

| | |
|---|---|
| וּתְפִלַּת צַדִּיקִים | *but prayer of righteous people* |
| יִשְׁמָע | *he hears/listens to/heeds* |
| | Qal Impf 3ms שמע |

---

A monarch's mind is meandering water in YHWH's grip;
he diverts it in whatever direction he wants.

PROV 21:1 ▪ DAY 161

# בִּרְצוֹת יְהוָה דַּרְכֵי־אִישׁ

| | |
|---:|:---|
| בִּרְצוֹת יְהוָה | *in/by/through/when pleasing of/to* **YHWH** |
| | בְּ prep + רצה Qal Inf Cst |
| דַּרְכֵי־אִישׁ | *ways/paths of man/person* |

# גַּם־אוֹיְבָיו יַשְׁלִם אִתּוֹ:

| | |
|---:|:---|
| ־גַּם | *even/also* |
| אוֹיְבָיו | *his enemies* |
| יַשְׁלִם | *he causes to be at peace* |
| | שלם Hiph Impf 3ms |
| אִתּוֹ | *with him* |

---

The human heart contemplates its course,
but it's YHWH who determines its movements.

PROV 16:9 ▪ DAY 162

תּוֹעֲבַ֣ת יְהוָ֑ה כָּל־גְּבַהּ־לֵֽב

| תּוֹעֲבַ֣ת יְהוָ֑ה | *abomination of* **YHWH** |
| כָּל־ | *every* |
| גְּבַהּ־לֵֽב | *one haughty/proud/arrogant of heart/mind* |

יָ֣ד לְיָ֑ד לֹ֣א יִנָּקֶֽה׃

| יָ֣ד | *hand* |
| לְיָ֑ד | *to hand* |
| לֹ֣א יִנָּקֶֽה | *he will not go unpunished* נקה Niph Impf 3ms |

---

YHWH stays away from malefactors,
but he pays attention to the prayers of the pious.

PROV 15:29 • DAY 163

שִׂפְתֵי צַדִּיק יִרְעוּ רַבִּים

| | |
|---|---|
| שִׂפְתֵי צַדִּיק | *lips of righteous person* |
| יִרְעוּ | *(they) shepherd/lead/nourish* |
| | Qal Impf 3mp רעה |
| רַבִּים | *many* |

וֶאֱוִילִים בַּחֲסַר־לֵב יָמוּתוּ׃

| | |
|---|---|
| וֶאֱוִילִים | *but fools* |
| בַּחֲסַר־לֵב | *in/by lack/want/deficiency of heart/mind/understanding/ conscience* |
| יָמוּתוּ | *(they) die* |
| | Qal Impf 3mp מות |

---

When a person's paths are pleasing to YHWH,
he'll even make amends with his enemies.

PROV 16:7 · DAY 164

בְּכָל־מָקוֹם עֵינֵי יְהוָה

| | |
|---|---|
| בְּכָל־מָקוֹם | *in every place* |
| עֵינֵי יְהוָה | *eyes of* **YHWH** |

צֹפוֹת רָעִים וְטוֹבִים:

| | |
|---|---|
| צֹפוֹת | *(ones that) watch* |
| | צפה Qal Ptcp fp |
| רָעִים | *evil/bad people* |
| וְטוֹבִים | *and good people* |

---

Everyone whose heart is haughty is an abomination to YHWH;
assuredly, such a one won't go unpunished.

PROV 16:5 ▪ DAY 165

לֹא־יְאֻנֶּה לַצַּדִּיק כָּל־אָ֑וֶן

| | |
|---|---|
| לֹא־יְאֻנֶּה | *(it) does not happen* |
| | Pual Impf 3ms אנה |
| לַצַּדִּיק | *to the righteous person* |
| כָּל־אָ֑וֶן | *any trouble/misfortune/harm/evil* |

וּרְשָׁעִים מָלְאוּ רָֽע׃

| | |
|---|---|
| וּרְשָׁעִים | *but wicked people* |
| מָלְאוּ | *(they) are filled with* |
| | Qal Pf 3cp מלא |
| רָע | *evil/harm/trouble/calamity* |

A moral man's lips lead many,
but dolts die from meagerness of mind.

PROV 10:21 ▪ DAY 166

דְּאָגָה בְלֶב־אִישׁ יַשְׁחֶנָּה

| | |
|---|---|
| דְּאָגָה | *anxiety/worry* |
| בְלֶב־אִישׁ | *in heart/mind of man/person* |
| יַשְׁחֶנָּה | *(it) weighs it down* |
| | Hiph Impf 3ms שחה + 3fs sx |

וְדָבָר טוֹב יְשַׂמְּחֶנָּה׃

| | |
|---|---|
| וְדָבָר | *but word* |
| טוֹב | *good/beneficial/pleasant* |
| יְשַׂמְּחֶנָּה | *(it) makes it joyful/glad/happy* |
| | Piel Impf 3ms שמח + 3fs sx |

---

YHWH's eyes are everywhere,
watching the vile and the pious.

PROV 15:3 ▪ DAY 167

יָתֵר מֵרֵעֵהוּ צַדִּיק

| | |
|---|---|
| יָתֵר | *let (him) seek out/search out/investigate* |
| | Hiph Juss 3ms תור |
| מֵרֵעֵהוּ | *(from) his friend/companion* |
| צַדִּיק | *righteous person* |

וְדֶרֶךְ רְשָׁעִים תַּתְעֵם:

| | |
|---|---|
| וְדֶרֶךְ רְשָׁעִים | *but way/path of wicked people* |
| תַּתְעֵם | *(it) leads them astray* |
| | Hiph Impf 3fs תעה + 3mp sx |

---

No misfortune befalls a meritorious man,
but the reprobate are replete with trouble.

PROV 12:21 ▪ DAY 168

כָּל־יְמֵי עָנִי רָעִים

| | |
|---|---|
| כָּל־יְמֵי עָנִי | *all days of*<br>*poor/afflicted/lowly/humble person* |
| רָעִים | *evil/bad/calamitous* |

וְטוֹב־לֵב מִשְׁתֶּה תָמִיד:

| | |
|---|---|
| וְטוֹב־לֵב | *but one good of*<br>*heart/mind* |
| מִשְׁתֶּה | *feast/banquet* |
| תָמִיד | *continuousness/perpetuity/*<br>*continually/perpetually* |

---

Worry weighs down one's heart,
but a helpful word makes it happy.

PROV 12:25 ▪ DAY 169

הֵן צַדִּיק בָּאָרֶץ יְשֻׁלָּם

| | |
|---|---|
| הֵן | *behold/if* |
| צַדִּיק | *righteous person* |
| בָּאָרֶץ | *on the earth* |
| יְשֻׁלָּם | *(he) is repaid/requited* |

Pual Impf 3ms שלם

אַף כִּי־רָשָׁע וְחוֹטֵא:

| | |
|---|---|
| אַף כִּי־ | *how much more* |
| רָשָׁע | *wicked/guilty person* |
| וְחוֹטֵא | *and one who sins/offends/wrongs* |

Qal Ptcp ms חטא + conj וְ

---

A righteous man seeks answers from his friend,
but the path of the rash leads them astray.

PROV 12:26 • DAY 170

# דְּבַר־שֶׁקֶר יִשְׂנָא צַדִּיק

| | |
|---|---|
| דְּבַר־שֶׁקֶר | *word/statement/speech of falsehood/deceit/untruth/fraudulence* |
| יִשְׂנָא | *(he) hates* <br> Qal Impf 3ms שׂנא |
| צַדִּיק | *righteous person* |

# וְרָשָׁע יַבְאִישׁ וְיַחְפִּיר:

| | |
|---|---|
| וְרָשָׁע | *but wicked person* |
| יַבְאִישׁ | *(he) becomes odious/foul // (he) makes himself odious/foul* <br> Hiph Impf 3ms באשׁ |
| וְיַחְפִּיר | *and (he) acts disgracefully/shamefully* <br> Hiph Impf 3ms חפר + conj וְ |

---

All the days of a victimized man are dreadful,
but he whose mind is placid has a perpetual banquet.

PROV 15:15 ▪ DAY 171

לְאָדָם מַעַרְכֵי־לֵב

| | |
|---|---|
| לְאָדָם | *to man/person/humankind/humanity* |
| מַעַרְכֵי־לֵב | *arrangements/orderliness/dispositions of heart/mind* |

וּמֵיהוָה מַעֲנֵה לָשׁוֹן:

| | |
|---|---|
| וּמֵיהוָה | *and/but from* YHWH |
| מַעֲנֵה לָשׁוֹן | *answer of tongue* |

---

If a righteous man is recompensed on earth,
how much more a sinister person and a sinner!

PROV 11:31 ▪ DAY 172

## יוֹדֵעַ צַדִּיק נֶפֶשׁ בְּהֶמְתּוֹ

| | |
|---|---|
| יוֹדֵעַ | *(one who) knows* |
| | Qal Ptcp ms ידע |
| צַדִּיק | *righteous person* |
| נֶפֶשׁ בְּהֶמְתּוֹ | *desire/appetite/soul of his cattle* |

## וְרַחֲמֵי רְשָׁעִים אַכְזָרִי:

| | |
|---|---|
| וְרַחֲמֵי רְשָׁעִים | *but compassions/mercies of wicked people* |
| אַכְזָרִי | *cruel/merciless* |

---

A decent man detests a deceptive statement,
but a petulant one is putrid and acts with turpitude.

PROV 13:5 ▪ DAY 173

חָמַד רָשָׁע מְצוֹד רָעִים

| חָמַד | *(he) desires/covets/takes pleasure in* |
| | Qal Pf 3ms חמד |

| רָשָׁע | *wicked person* |

| מְצוֹד רָעִים | *catch/snare of*<br>*evil/bad people* |

וְשֹׁרֶשׁ צַדִּיקִים יִתֵּן:

| וְשֹׁרֶשׁ צַדִּיקִים | *but root of*<br>*righteous people* |

| יִתֵּן | *(it) will produce* |
| | Qal Impf 3ms נתן |

---

The heart's dispositions are of man,
but the tongue's declaration is from YHWH.

PROV 16:1 ▪ DAY 174

## לַחֲכַם־לֵב יִקָּרֵא נָבֹ֖ון

לַחֲכַם־לֵב    *one wise/sage of*
*heart/mind*

יִקָּרֵא    *(he) will be called/proclaimed*
Niph Impf 3ms קרא

נָבֹ֖ון    *one who is understanding/discerning/*
*perceptive/intelligent*
Niph Ptcp ms בין

## וּמֶתֶק שְׂפָתַיִם יֹסִיף לֶקַח׃

וּמֶתֶק שְׂפָתַיִם    *and sweetness of*
*lips*

יֹסִיף    *(it) adds/increases*
Hiph Impf 3ms יסף

לֶקַח    *learning/teaching*

---

A kind man is conscious of his cattle's appetite,
but the compassions of criminals are cruel.

PROV 12:10 ▪ DAY 175

## לְפִי־שִׂכְלוֹ יְהֻלַּל־אִישׁ

| לְפִי־שִׂכְלוֹ | *for mouth of/on account of/in accordance with his prudence/wisdom/ understanding* |
|---|---|
| יְהֻלַּל־ | *(he) will be praised* <br> Pual Impf 3ms הלל |
| אִישׁ | *man/person* |

## וְנַעֲוֵה־לֵב יִהְיֶה לָבוּז׃

| וְנַעֲוֵה־לֵב | *but one who is twisted/perverse of heart/mind* <br> Niph Ptcp ms עוה + conj וְ |
|---|---|
| יִהְיֶה | *(he) will be/become* <br> Qal Impf 3ms היה |
| לָבוּז | *(for) contempt/laughingstock* |

---

A mischievous man covets the catch of the corrupt,
but the root of the righteous will produce.

PROV 12:12 ▪ DAY 176

## צַדִּיק אֹכֵל לְשֹׂבַע נַפְשׁוֹ

| | |
|---|---|
| צַדִּיק | *righteous person* |
| אֹכֵל | *(one who) eats* |
| | Qal Ptcp ms אכל |
| לְשֹׂבַע נַפְשׁוֹ | *for satisfaction/satiation of his appetite/desire* |

## וּבֶטֶן רְשָׁעִים תֶּחְסָר׃

| | |
|---|---|
| וּבֶטֶן רְשָׁעִים | *but stomach/belly of wicked people* |
| תֶּחְסָר | *(it) lacks* |
| | Qal Impf 3fs חסר |

---

One whose mind is enlightened will be called learned,
and mellifluous lips increase culture.

PROV 16:21 ▪ DAY 177

# מְגוֹרַת רָשָׁע הִיא תְבוֹאֶנּוּ

מְגוֹרַת רָשָׁע    *fear/terror/dread of*
           *wicked/guilty person*

הִיא    *it/that*

תְבוֹאֶנּוּ    *(it) will come upon him*
     Qal Impf 3fs בוא + 3ms sx

# וְתַאֲוַת צַדִּיקִים יִתֵּן׃

וְתַאֲוַת צַדִּיקִים    *but desire/longing of*
           *righteous people*

יִתֵּן    *he will give/grant/produce*
     Qal Impf 3ms נתן

---

A person is praised in accordance with his erudition,
but one whose mind is distorted is a laughingstock.

PROV 12:8 ▪ DAY 178

בֵּית צַדִּיק חֹסֶן רָב

| | |
|---|---|
| בֵּית צַדִּיק | *house/home of righteous person* |
| חֹסֶן | *treasure/wealth* |
| רָב | *much/great/abundant* |

וּבִתְבוּאַת רָשָׁע נֶעְכָּרֶת:

| | |
|---|---|
| וּבִתְבוּאַת רָשָׁע | *but in/with/by income/yield/produce of wicked person* |
| נֶעְכָּרֶת | *(that which) is troubled* |
| | Niph Ptcp fs עכר |

---

An excellent man eats his fill,
but the paunch of the profligate will be empty.

PROV 13:25 ▪ DAY 179

לָמָּה־זֶּה מְחִיר בְּיַד־כְּסִיל

| | |
|---:|:---|
| לָמָּה־ | *why?* |
| זֶּה | *this* |
| מְחִיר | *price* |
| בְּיַד־כְּסִיל | *in hand of fool/dolt/idiot* |

לִקְנוֹת חָכְמָה וְלֶב־אָיִן:

| | |
|---:|:---|
| לִקְנוֹת | *to buy/acquire/obtain*<br>לְ prep + קנה Qal Inf Cst |
| חָכְמָה | *wisdom* |
| וְלֶב־ | *and/but heart/mind/understanding/ conscience* |
| אָיִן | *there is not* |

---

What a diabolical man dreads will come upon him,
but he will grant the desire of the righteous.

PROV 10:24 ▪ DAY 180

# יִרְאַת יְהוָה תּוֹסִיף יָמִים

| | |
|---:|:---|
| יִרְאַת יְהוָה | *fear/awe/reverence of* **YHWH** |
| תּוֹסִיף | *(it) adds/increases* <br> יסף Hiph Impf 3fs |
| יָמִים | *days* |

# וּשְׁנוֹת רְשָׁעִים תִּקְצֹרְנָה׃

| | |
|---:|:---|
| וּשְׁנוֹת רְשָׁעִים | *but years/[sleeps] of wicked/guilty people* |
| תִּקְצֹרְנָה | *(they) will be short/shortened* <br> קצר Qal Impf 3fp |

---

A holy man's house has vast wealth,
but an infernal man's income involves affliction.

PROV 15:6 ▪ DAY 181

מְסִלַּת יְשָׁרִים סוּר מֵרָע

| מְסִלַּת יְשָׁרִים | *highway/road of upright people* |
|---|---|
| סוּר | *to turn away/aside* <br> Qal Inf Cst סור |
| מֵרָע | *from evil* |

שֹׁמֵר נַפְשׁוֹ נֹצֵר דַּרְכּוֹ:

| שֹׁמֵר | *one who guards/keeps/preserves/ protects* <br> Qal Ptcp ms שמר |
|---|---|
| נַפְשׁוֹ | *his soul/life/self* |
| נֹצֵר | *one who guards/protects/preserves* <br> Qal Ptcp ms נצר |
| דַּרְכּוֹ | *his way/path* |

---

Why is this sum in an oaf's fist,
for acquiring wisdom in the absence of understanding?

PROV 17:16 • DAY 182

הָפְוֹךְ רְשָׁעִים וְאֵינָם

| הָפְוֹךְ | *overthrowing* |
|---|---|
| | Qal Inf Abs הפך |

| רְשָׁעִים | *wicked people* |
|---|---|

| וְאֵינָם | *and they are not* |
|---|---|

וּבֵית צַדִּיקִים יַעֲמֹד:

| וּבֵית צַדִּיקִים | *but house/household/home/family/ dynasty of* |
|---|---|
| | *righteous people* |

| יַעֲמֹד | *(it) will stand/endure* |
|---|---|
| | Qal Impf 3ms עמד |

---

Revering YHWH adds to one's days,
but the years of rogues will be reduced.

PROV 10:27 ▪ DAY 183

רוּם־עֵינַיִם וּרְחַב־לֵב

| רוּם־עֵינַיִם | *haughtiness of eyes* |
|---|---|
| וּרְחַב־לֵב | *and one broad of heart/mind* |

נֵר רְשָׁעִים חַטָּאת:

| נֵר רְשָׁעִים | *lamp/untilled land of wicked people* |
|---|---|
| חַטָּאת | *sin* |

> The high road of the upright is to eschew perversity;
> he who cares about his soul preserves his path.
>
> PROV 16:17 ▪ DAY 184

בְּרָעָתוֹ יִדָּחֶה רָשָׁע

בְּרָעָתוֹ  *in/by his evil*

יִדָּחֶה  *(he) is overthrown/thrust down*
Niph Impf 3ms דחה

רָשָׁע  *wicked person*

וְחֹסֶה בְמוֹתוֹ צַדִּיק:

וְחֹסֶה  *and/but (one who) takes refuge/shelter*
Qal Ptcp ms חסה + conj וְ

בְמוֹתוֹ  *in his death*

צַדִּיק  *righteous person*

---

The unscrupulous are overthrown and are no more,
but the house of the honest will last.

PROV 12:7 • DAY 185

מֵיהוָה מִצְעֲדֵי־גָבֶר

| | |
|---|---|
| מֵיהוָה | *from* YHWH |
| מִצְעֲדֵי־גָבֶר | *steps of man* |

וְאָדָם מַה־יָּבִין דַּרְכּוֹ:

| | |
|---|---|
| וְאָדָם | *and/but man/person/humankind/ humanity* |
| מַה־ | *how?* |
| יָּבִין | *can (he/it) understand/discern/ perceive* |
| | Qal Impf 3ms בין |
| דַּרְכּוֹ | *his/its way/path* |

---

Haughty eyes and a hubristic heart—
sin is in the virgin soil of the villainous.

PROV 21:4 • DAY 186

# דִּבְרֵי רְשָׁעִים אֱרָב־דָּם

| | |
|---|---|
| דִּבְרֵי רְשָׁעִים | *words of*<br>   *wicked people* |
| אֱרָב־ | *lie in wait/ambush // to lie in wait/to*<br>*ambush*<br>Qal Impv ms ארב<br>Qal Inf Cst ארב |
| דָּם | *blood* |

# וּפִי יְשָׁרִים יַצִּילֵם:

| | |
|---|---|
| וּפִי יְשָׁרִים | *but mouth of*<br>   *upright people* |
| יַצִּילֵם | *(it) delivers/rescues them*<br>Hiph Impf 3ms נצל + 3mp sx |

---

A devilish man is overthrown by his evil,
and a righteous man takes refuge in his demise.

PROV 14:32  •  DAY 187

כַּעֲבֹר סוּפָה וְאֵין רָשָׁע

כַּעֲבוֹר סוּפָה    *as/when passing by/on/over of storm/whirlwind*

כְּ prep + עבר Qal Inf Cst

וְאֵין    *and there is not*

רָשָׁע    *wicked person*

וְצַדִּיק יְסוֹד עוֹלָם׃

וְצַדִּיק    *but righteous person*

יְסוֹד עוֹלָם    *foundation of long duration/unendingness/eternity*

---

A person's steps are from YHWH;
how, then, can a man fathom his path?

PROV 20:24 ▪ DAY 188

## חֲטָאִים תְּרַדֶּף רָעָה

| | |
|---|---|
| חֲטָאִים | *sinners* |
| תְּרַדֶּף | *(it) pursues* |
| | רדף Piel Impf 3fs |
| רָעָה | *evil/harm/trouble/calamity/disaster* |

## וְאֶת־צַדִּיקִים יְשַׁלֶּם־טוֹב:

| | |
|---|---|
| וְאֶת־צַדִּיקִים | *but righteous people* |
| יְשַׁלֶּם־ | *he repays/rewards/requites* |
| | שלם Piel Impf 3ms |
| טוֹב | *good/goodness/benefit* |

---

The declaration of the diabolical: "Get ready for bloodshed!"
But the mouth of the virtuous delivers them.

PROV 12:6 ▪ DAY 189

## מְאוֹר־עֵינַיִם יְשַׂמַּח־לֵב

| | |
|---:|:---|
| מְאוֹר־עֵינַיִם | *light of eyes* |
| יְשַׂמַּח־ | *(it) makes joyful/glad/happy/ [irradiates]* |
| | Piel Impf 3ms שׂמח |
| לֵב | *heart/mind* |

## שְׁמוּעָה טוֹבָה תְּדַשֶּׁן־עָצֶם:

| | |
|---:|:---|
| שְׁמוּעָה | *report/news* |
| טוֹבָה | *good/beneficial/pleasant* |
| תְּדַשֶּׁן־ | *(it) fattens* |
| | Piel Impf 3fs דשׁן |
| עָצֶם | *bone* |

---

When the storm dies down, the wicked man is no more;
but a principled person has a perdurable foundation.

PROV 10:25 • DAY 190

מַ֥יִם עֲמֻקִּים֮ דִּבְרֵ֪י פִי־אִ֥ישׁ

| מַ֥יִם | water/waters |
| עֲמֻקִּים | deep |
| דִּבְרֵ֪י פִי־אִ֥ישׁ | words of<br>mouth of<br>man/person |

נַ֥חַל נֹ֝בֵ֗עַ מְק֥וֹר חָכְמָֽה׃

| נַ֥חַל | wadi/stream |
| נֹ֝בֵ֗עַ | (one) that gushes<br>Qal Ptcp ms נבע |
| מְק֥וֹר חָכְמָֽה | fountain/spring/source of<br>wisdom |

## פּוֹרֵעַ מוּסָר מוֹאֵס נַפְשׁוֹ

| פּוֹרֵעַ | *one who ignores/avoids* |
|---|---|
| | Qal Ptcp ms פרע |

| מוּסָר | *instruction/training/education/warning/* |
|---|---|
| | *discipline/correction/chastisement* |

| מוֹאֵס | *one who rejects/despises* |
|---|---|
| | Qal Ptcp ms מאס |

| נַפְשׁוֹ | *his soul/life/self* |
|---|---|

## וְשׁוֹמֵעַ תּוֹכַחַת קוֹנֶה לֵּב׃

| וְשׁוֹמֵעַ | *but one who hears/listens to/heeds* |
|---|---|
| | Qal Ptcp ms שמע + conj וְ |

| תּוֹכַחַת | *reproof/rebuke* |
|---|---|

| קוֹנֶה | *one who acquires/gets/gains/obtains* |
|---|---|
| | Qal Ptcp ms קנה |

| לֵב | *heart/mind/understanding/conscience* |
|---|---|

---

The light of the eyes makes the heart happy;
a good report puts meat on the bone.

PROV 15:30 • DAY 192

טוֹב־מְעַט בְּיִרְאַת יְהוָה

| | |
|---|---|
| טוֹב־ | *better* |
| מְעַט | *little* |
| בְּיִרְאַת יְהוָה | *with fear/awe/reverence of* **YHWH** |

מֵאוֹצָר רָב וּמְהוּמָה בוֹ:

| | |
|---|---|
| מֵאוֹצָר | *than treasure* |
| רָב | *much/great/abundant* |
| וּמְהוּמָה | *and confusion/turmoil/tumult* |
| בוֹ | *with it* |

> The words of a man's mouth are deep waters,
> a gushing stream, a spring of wisdom.
>
> PROV 18:4 ▪ DAY 193

בְּפִי־אֱוִיל חֹטֶר גַּאֲוָה

| | |
|---|---|
| בְּפִי־אֱוִיל | *in mouth of*<br>*fool* |
| חֹטֶר גַּאֲוָה | *rod of*<br>*haughtiness/pride* |

וְשִׂפְתֵי חֲכָמִים תִּשְׁמוּרֵם:

| | |
|---|---|
| וְשִׂפְתֵי חֲכָמִים | *but lips of*<br>*wise/sage people* |
| תִּשְׁמוּרֵם | *(they) guard/keep/preserve/protect*<br>*them* |

Qal Impf 3fs(!) שמר + 3mp sx

One who ignores instruction rejects himself,
but he who listens to criticism acquires a conscience.

PROV 15:32 ▪ DAY 194

# כָּל־עָרוּם יַעֲשֶׂה בְדַעַת

כָּל־עָרוּם   *every prudent/shrewd/clever person*

יַעֲשֶׂה   *(he) acts*
Qal Impf 3ms עשׂה

בְדַעַת   *with knowledge*

# וּכְסִיל יִפְרְשׂ אִוֶּלֶת׃

וּכְסִיל   *but fool/dolt/idiot*

יִפְרְשׂ   *(he) spreads out*
Qal Impf 3ms פרשׂ

אִוֶּלֶת   *folly*

---

Better an iota with the awe of YHWH
than troves of treasure with turmoil in tow.

PROV 15:16 • DAY 195

אָדָם חֲסַר־לֵב תּוֹקֵעַ כָּף

| | |
|---|---|
| אָדָם | *man/person* |
| חֲסַר־לֵב | *lacking/devoid of heart/mind/understanding/conscience* |
| תּוֹקֵעַ | *(one who) strikes/clasps* <br> Qal Ptcp ms תקע |
| כָּף | *hand* |

עֹרֵב עֲרֻבָּה לִפְנֵי רֵעֵהוּ:

| | |
|---|---|
| עֹרֵב | *one who pledges* <br> Qal Ptcp ms ערב |
| עֲרֻבָּה | *pledge of surety* |
| לִפְנֵי רֵעֵהוּ | *before his neighbor/friend/companion* |

---

A proud rod is in a dolt's mouth,
but the lips of the learned preserve them.

PROV 14:3 • DAY 196

מַיִם עֲמֻקִּים עֵצָה בְלֶב־אִישׁ

| מַיִם | water/waters |
| עֲמֻקִּים | deep |
| עֵצָה | counsel/plan/purpose/plot/decision/<br>struggle/doubt |
| בְלֶב־אִישׁ | in heart/mind of<br>man/person |

וְאִישׁ תְּבוּנָה יִדְלֶנָּה:

| וְאִישׁ תְּבוּנָה | and/but man/person of<br>understanding/discernment |
| יִדְלֶנָּה | (he) will draw it<br>Qal Impf 3ms דלה + 3fs sx |

---

Every shrewd man acts with skill,
but a numbskull disseminates stupidity.

PROV 13:16 ▪ DAY 197

מִגְדַּל־עֹז שֵׁם יְהֹוָה

מִגְדַּל־עֹז    *tower of strength*

שֵׁם יְהֹוָה    *name of* **YHWH**

בּוֹ־יָרוּץ צַדִּיק וְנִשְׂגָּב׃

בּוֹ־    *into it*

יָרוּץ    *(he) runs*
Qal Impf 3ms רוץ

צַדִּיק    *righteous person*

וְנִשְׂגָּב    *and/then he is inaccessible*
Niph weqatal 3ms שׂגב

A person devoid of understanding shakes hands,
pledging surety before his neighbor.

PROV 17:18 ▪ DAY 198

בְּפֶּה חָנֵף יַשְׁחִת רֵעֵהוּ

| | |
|---|---|
| בְּפֶּה | *with mouth* |
| חָנֵף | *godless/impious person* |
| יַשְׁחִת | *(he) destroys/corrupts* |
| | Hiph Impf 3ms שחת |
| רֵעֵהוּ | *his neighbor/friend/companion* |

וּבְדַעַת צַדִּיקִים יֵחָלֵצוּ:

| | |
|---|---|
| וּבְדַעַת | *but by knowledge* |
| צַדִּיקִים | *righteous people* |
| יֵחָלֵצוּ | *(they) are delivered/rescued* |
| | Niph Impf 3mp חלץ |

---

The deliberation of a man's mind is deep water,
but a discerning person can draw it.

PROV 20:5 ▪ DAY 199

מַצְרֵף לַכֶּסֶף וְכוּר לַזָּהָב

מַצְרֵף      *crucible*

לַכֶּסֶף     *for the silver*

וְכוּר       *and furnace*

לַזָּהָב      *for the gold*

וּבֹחֵן לִבּוֹת יְהֹוָה:

וּבֹחֵן      *and/but (one who) tests/examines*

        Qal Ptcp ms בחן + conj וְ

לִבּוֹת     *hearts/minds/consciences*

יְהֹוָה     *YHWH*

---

YHWH's name is a strong fortress;
a virtuous man runs into it and is invincible.

PROV 18:10 • DAY 200

# נֹצֵר פִּיו שֹׁמֵר נַפְשׁוֹ

| | |
|---|---|
| נֹצֵר | *one who guards/protects/preserves* |
| | Qal Ptcp ms נצר |
| פִּיו | *his mouth* |
| שֹׁמֵר | *one who guards/keeps/preserves/ protects* |
| | Qal Ptcp ms שמר |
| נַפְשׁוֹ | *his soul/life/self* |

# פֹּשֵׂק שְׂפָתָיו מְחִתָּה־לוֹ׃

| | |
|---|---|
| פֹּשֵׂק | *one who opens wide* |
| | Qal Ptcp ms פשק |
| שְׂפָתָיו | *his lips* |
| מְחִתָּה־ | *ruin/terror* |
| לוֹ | *to/for him* |

An impious person corrupts his companion with his mouth,
but the virtuous are delivered by knowledge.

PROV 11:9 ▪ DAY 201

בְּחֶסֶד וֶאֱמֶת יְכֻפַּר עָוֹן

בְּחֶסֶד וֶאֱמֶת     *with/by/through loyalty/steadfast love/*
*lovingkindness/faithfulness/probity*
*and truth/honesty/trustworthiness/*
*faithfulness*

יְכֻפַּר     *(it) is atoned for*
      כפר Pual Impf 3ms

עָוֹן     *iniquity/offense/sin*

וּבְיִרְאַת יְהֹוָה סוּר מֵרָע:

וּבְיִרְאַת יְהֹוָה     *and in/by/through fear/awe/reverence of*
**YHWH**

סוּר     *to turn away/aside*
      סור Qal Inf Cst

מֵרָע     *from evil*

---

A crucible for silver and a furnace for gold,
but YHWH tests hearts.

PROV 17:3 ▪ DAY 202

בְּטוּב צַדִּיקִים תַּעֲלֹץ קִרְיָה

בְּטוּב צַדִּיקִים    *in good/goodness/prosperity of*
                    *righteous people*

תַּעֲלֹץ    *(it) rejoices/exults*
           Qal Impf 3fs עלץ

קִרְיָה    *city*

וּבַאֲבֹד רְשָׁעִים רִנָּה:

וּבַאֲבֹד רְשָׁעִים    *and in perishing/destruction of*
                     *wicked people*
                     Qal Inf Cst אבד + prep בְּ + conj וְ

רִנָּה    *rejoicing/cries of joy*

---

One who watches his mouth maintains his life;
opening wide one's lips leads to ruin.

PROV 13:3 ▪ DAY 203

## צַדִּיק לְעוֹלָם בַּל־יִמּוֹט

| | |
|---|---|
| צַדִּיק | *righteous person* |
| לְעוֹלָם | *for long duration/forever* |
| בַּל־יִמּוֹט | *(he) will not be moved/shaken* |
| | Niph Impf 3ms מוט |

## וּרְשָׁעִים לֹא יִשְׁכְּנוּ־אָרֶץ:

| | |
|---|---|
| וּרְשָׁעִים | *but wicked people* |
| לֹא יִשְׁכְּנוּ־ | *(they) will not dwell/inhabit/settle* |
| | Qal Impf 3mp שכן |
| אָרֶץ | *land* |

> It's through authenticity and truth that iniquity is atoned for,
> and it's through revering YHWH that one repents from evil.
>
> PROV 16:6 ▪ DAY 204

## נֵר יְהוָה נִשְׁמַת אָדָם

נֵר יְהוָה    *lamp of*
**YHWH**

נִשְׁמַת אָדָם    *breath/spirit of*
*man/person/humankind/humanity*

## חֹפֵשׂ כָּל־חַדְרֵי־בָטֶן:

חֹפֵשׂ    *one that searches out*
Qal Ptcp ms חפשׂ

כָּל־חַדְרֵי־בָטֶן    *all rooms/chambers of*
*belly/abdomen/stomach*

---

A city exults when the honorable do well,
and when the villainous expire—cries of joy!

PROV 11:10 • DAY 205

בְּבִרְכַּת יְשָׁרִים תָּרוּם קָרֶת

| | |
|---:|:---|
| בְּבִרְכַּת יְשָׁרִים | *in/by/through blessing of upright people* |
| תָּרוּם | *(it) is exalted* |
| | Qal Impf 3fs רום |
| קָרֶת | *city* |

וּבְפִי רְשָׁעִים תֵּהָרֵס:

| | |
|---:|:---|
| וּבְפִי רְשָׁעִים | *but by/through mouth of wicked people* |
| תֵּהָרֵס | *it is overthrown/torn down* |
| | Niph Impf 3fs הרס |

---

A righteous man won't ever be eradicated,
but the lawless can't dwell in the land.

PROV 10:30 ▪ DAY 206

זֵכֶר צַדִּיק לִבְרָכָה

| | |
|---|---|
| זֵכֶר צַדִּיק | *memory/remembrance/mention of righteous person* |
| לִבְרָכָה | *for blessing* |

וְשֵׁם רְשָׁעִים יִרְקָב׃

| | |
|---|---|
| וְשֵׁם רְשָׁעִים | *but name of wicked people* |
| יִרְקָב | *(it) will rot/decay* |
| | רקב Qal Impf 3ms |

---

A man's breath is YHWH's lamp,
investigating the abdomen's every cavity.

PROV 20:27 ▪ DAY 207

חֲנֹ֣ךְ לַנַּ֭עַר עַל־פִּ֣י דַרְכּ֑וֹ

| חֲנֹ֣ךְ | train/dedicate |
| | Qal Impv ms חנך |

| לַנַּ֭עַר | the young person/child |

| עַל־פִּ֣י דַרְכּ֑וֹ | according to (the command/dictate of) his way/path/road |

גַּ֥ם כִּֽי־יַ֝זְקִ֗ין לֹֽא־יָס֥וּר מִמֶּֽנָּה׃

| גַּ֥ם כִּֽי־ | even/also when |

| יַ֝זְקִ֗ין | he is old |
| | Hiph Impf 3ms זקן |

| לֹֽא־יָס֥וּר | he will not turn away/aside |
| | Qal Impf 3ms סור |

| מִמֶּֽנָּה | from it |

---

A city is exalted by the blessing of the honorable,
but by the mouth of libertines it is obliterated.

PROV 11:11 ▪ DAY 208

פִּי־צַדִּיק יָנוּב חָכְמָה

| | |
|---|---|
| פִּי־צַדִּיק | *mouth of* |
| | *righteous person* |

| | |
|---|---|
| יָנוּב | *(it) produces* |
| | Qal Impf 3ms נוב |

| | |
|---|---|
| חָכְמָה | *wisdom* |

וּלְשׁוֹן תַּהְפֻּכוֹת תִּכָּרֵת׃

| | |
|---|---|
| וּלְשׁוֹן תַּהְפֻּכוֹת | *but tongue of* |
| | *perversities* |

| | |
|---|---|
| תִּכָּרֵת | *(it) will be cut off* |
| | Niph Impf 3fs כרת |

The mention of a righteous man results in blessing,
but the name of the depraved will rot.

PROV 10:7 ▪ DAY 209

## גַּם בְּלֹא־דַעַת נֶפֶשׁ לֹא־טֽוֹב

| | |
|---|---|
| גַּם | *even as* |
| בְּלֹא־דַעַת | *without knowledge* |
| נֶפֶשׁ | *soul/person/desire/appetite* |
| ־לֹא | *not* |
| טֽוֹב | *good/beneficial* |

## וְאָץ בְּרַגְלַיִם חוֹטֵֽא:

| | |
|---|---|
| וְאָץ | *and/so one who hurries/is hasty* |
| | Qal Ptcp ms אוץ + conj וְ |
| בְּרַגְלַיִם | *with feet* |
| חוֹטֵֽא | *one who sins/offends/wrongs/misses the mark* |
| | Qal Ptcp ms חטא |

---

Give a youth over to his path;
then, when he's old, he won't turn away from it.

PROV 22:6 ▪ DAY 210

## הוֹלֵךְ בְּיָשְׁרוֹ יְרֵא יְהוָה

הוֹלֵךְ — *one who walks*
הלך Qal Ptcp ms

בְּיָשְׁרוֹ — *in his uprightness/integrity*

יְרֵא יְהוָה — *one fearful/reverent/respectful of*
**YHWH**

## וּנְלוֹז דְּרָכָיו בּוֹזֵהוּ׃

וּנְלוֹז דְּרָכָיו — *but one who is devious of/in his ways/paths*
וְ + לוז Niph Ptcp ms + conj

בּוֹזֵהוּ — *one who despises him*
בזה Qal Ptcp ms + 3ms sx

---

A righteous man's mouth produces progress,
but a petulant tongue will be cut off.

PROV 10:31 ▪ DAY 211

מָעוֹז לַתֹּם דֶּרֶךְ יְהֹוָה

| | |
|---|---|
| מָעוֹז | *stronghold/fortress/refuge* |
| לַתֹּם | *to/for the integrity/innocence/* *blamelessness/purity/perfection* |
| דֶּרֶךְ יְהֹוָה | *way/path of* **YHWH** |

וּמְחִתָּה לְפֹעֲלֵי אָוֶן׃

| | |
|---|---|
| וּמְחִתָּה | *but ruin/terror* |
| לְפֹעֲלֵי | *to/for ones who work/practice* לְ prep + פעל Qal Ptcp mp |
| אָוֶן | *iniquity/injustice/sin/evil* |

---

Just as desire without awareness goes awry,
one who's hasty with his feet misses the mark.

PROV 19:2 ▪ DAY 212

רָשָׁע עֹשֶׂה פְעֻלַּת־שָׁקֶר

| רָשָׁע | *wicked person* |
|---|---|
| עֹשֶׂה | *(one who) makes* |
| | Qal Ptcp ms עשׂה |
| פְעֻלַּת־שָׁקֶר | *wage of* |
| | *falsehood/deceit/untruth/fraudulence* |

וְזֹרֵעַ צְדָקָה שֶׂכֶר אֱמֶת:

| וְזֹרֵעַ | *but one who sows* |
|---|---|
| | Qal Ptcp ms זרע + conj וְ |
| צְדָקָה | *righteousness/truthfulness/justice* |
| שֶׂכֶר אֱמֶת | *pay/reward of* |
| | *truth/honesty/trustworthiness/* |
| | *faithfulness* |

---

One who acts with virtue venerates YHWH,
but one of perfidious proclivities despises him.

PROV 14:2 ▪ DAY 213

בַּחֵיק יוּטַל אֶת־הַגּוֹרָל

| | |
|---|---|
| בַּחֵיק | *into the lap* |
| יוּטַל | *(it) is cast* |
| | טול Hoph Impf 3ms |
| אֶת־הַגּוֹרָל | *the lot* |

וּמֵיהוָה כָּל־מִשְׁפָּטוֹ׃

| | |
|---|---|
| וּמֵיהוָה | *and/but from* YHWH |
| כָּל־מִשְׁפָּטוֹ | *every judgment/decision of it* |

---

YHWH's way is a refuge for the perfect
but a nightmare for malefactors.

PROV 10:29 ▪ DAY 214

פֶּ֤לֶס ׀ וּמֹאזְנֵ֣י מִשְׁפָּט֮ לַֽיהוָ֥ה

| פֶּ֤לֶס ׀ | balance/scale |
| וּמֹאזְנֵ֣י מִשְׁפָּט֮ | and scales/balances of justice/judgment |
| לַֽיהוָ֥ה | to YHWH |

מַ֝עֲשֵׂ֗הוּ כָּל־אַבְנֵי־כִֽיס׃

| מַ֝עֲשֵׂ֗הוּ | his work/handiwork |
| כָּל־אַבְנֵי־כִֽיס | all stones/weights of bag |

> A wicked man makes a dishonest wage,
> but he who sows virtue will reap a right reward.
>
> PROV 11:18 ▪ DAY 215

## אֶת־פְּנֵי מֵבִין חָכְמָה

אֶת־פְּנֵי מֵבִין     *with face of*
*one who understands/discerns/*
*perceives*

     Hiph Ptcp ms בין

חָכְמָה     *wisdom*

## וְעֵינֵי כְסִיל בִּקְצֵה־אָרֶץ׃

וְעֵינֵי כְסִיל     *but eyes of*
*fool/dolt/idiot*

בִּקְצֵה־אָרֶץ     *at end/edge of*
*earth*

---

The lot is cast into the lap,
but its every result is from YHWH.

PROV 16:33 ▪ DAY 216

מְזָרֶה רְשָׁעִים מֶלֶךְ חָכָם

מְזָרֶה   (one who) scatters/winnows/discerns

Piel Ptcp ms זרה

רְשָׁעִים   wicked/guilty people

מֶלֶךְ   king/ruler

חָכָם   wise/sage

וַיָּשֶׁב עֲלֵיהֶם אוֹפָן:

וַיָּשֶׁב   then he made return/made turn

Hiph wayyiqtol 3ms שׁוּב

עֲלֵיהֶם   on/upon/over them

אוֹפָן   wheel

The ledger and equable balances belong to YHWH;
all the weights in the purse are his handiwork.

PROV 16:11 ▪ DAY 217

# חוֹשֵׂךְ אֲמָרָיו יוֹדֵעַ דָּעַת

חוֹשֵׂךְ    *one who restrains/withholds/holds back*

    Qal Ptcp ms חשׂךְ

אֲמָרָיו    *his words*

יוֹדֵעַ    *one who knows*

    Qal Ptcp ms ידע

דָּעַת    *knowledge*


# יְקַר־רֹוּחַ אִישׁ תְּבוּנָה:

יְקַר־רֹוּחַ    *precious* [KETIV: *and cool*] *of*
        *spirit*

    וקר־רֹוּחַ  KETIV

אִישׁ תְּבוּנָה    *man/person of*
        *understanding/discernment*


Wisdom is visible in a shrewd man's mien,
but the eyes of a blockhead are on the horizon.

PROV 17:24 ▪ DAY 218

שֹׁד־רְשָׁעִים יְגוֹרֵם

שֹׁד־רְשָׁעִים     *violence of*
             *wicked people*

יְגוֹרֵם     *(it) drags/sweeps them away*
          Qal Impf 3ms גרר + 3mp sx

כִּי מֵאֲנוּ לַעֲשׂוֹת מִשְׁפָּט׃

כִּי     *for/because*

מֵאֲנוּ     *they refuse*
         Piel Pf 3cp מאן

לַעֲשׂוֹת     *to do/practice/execute*
         Qal Inf Cst עשׂה + prep לְ

מִשְׁפָּט     *justice*

---

A wise sovereign winnows the wicked;
then he rolls a wheel back and forth over them.

PROV 20:26 ▪ DAY 219

## לֵב יוֹדֵעַ מָרַת נַפְשׁוֹ

| | |
|---|---|
| לֵב | *heart/mind* |
| יוֹדֵעַ | *(one that) knows* |
| | Qal Ptcp ms ידע |
| מָרַת נַפְשׁוֹ | *bitterness of its soul/self* |

## וּבְשִׂמְחָתוֹ לֹא־יִתְעָרַב זָר:

| | |
|---|---|
| וּבְשִׂמְחָתוֹ | *and with/in/into its joy/gladness/ happiness/pleasure/mirth* |
| לֹא־יִתְעָרַב | *(he) cannot mix himself/enter* |
| | Hith Impf 3ms ערב |
| זָר | *stranger* |

---

He who spares his words displays decorum,
and a discerning man has a calm demeanor.

PROV 17:27 ▪ DAY 220

# שׁוּחָה עֲמֻקָּה פִּי זָרוֹת

שׁוּחָה    *pit*

עֲמֻקָּה    *deep*

פִּי זָרוֹת    *mouth of*
*strange women*

# זְעוּם יְהוָֹה יִפָּל־שָׁם:

זְעוּם יְהוָֹה    *one who is cursed of/by*
**YHWH**

Qal Pass Ptcp ms זעם

יִפָּל־    *(he) falls*

Qal Impf 3ms נפל

KETIV יפול־

שָׁם    *there*

---

The violence of the vile sweeps them away,
for they refuse to act with rectitude.

PROV 21:7 ▪ DAY 221

הֲפַכְפַּךְ דֶּרֶךְ אִישׁ וָזָר

| הֲפַכְפַּךְ | crooked/perverse |
| דֶּרֶךְ אִישׁ | way of man/person |
| וָזָר | guilty |

וְזַךְ יָשָׁר פָּעֳלוֹ׃

| וְזַךְ | but pure person |
| יָשָׁר | upright/right/correct |
| פָּעֳלוֹ | his conduct/work |

The soul's sadness only the heart understands,
nor can a stranger participate in its joy.

PROV 14:10 ▪ DAY 222

חָכָם יָרֵא וְסָר מֵרָע

חָכָם     *wise/sage person*

יָרֵא     *(one who) is reverent/cautious*

       Qal Ptcp ms ירא

וְסָר     *and (one who) turns away/aside*

       Qal Ptcp ms סור + conj וְ

מֵרָע     *from evil*

וּכְסִיל מִתְעַבֵּר וּבוֹטֵחַ:

וּכְסִיל     *but fool/dolt/idiot*

מִתְעַבֵּר     *(one who) is full of rage/wrath // makes
angry // delays/interferes*

       Hith Ptcp ms עבר

וּבוֹטֵחַ     *and (one who) trusts // is confident/
secure // falls*

       Qal Ptcp ms בטח + conj וְ

---

The maw of the meretricious is a gaping gulch;
he who is anathema to YHWH tumbles into it.

PROV 22:14  ▪  DAY 223

חֲכָמִים יִצְפְּנוּ־דָעַת

| חֲכָמִים | wise/sage people |
| יִצְפְּנוּ־ | (they) store/treasure up |
| | צפן Qal Impf 3mp |
| דָעַת | knowledge |

וּפִי־אֱוִיל מְחִתָּה קְרֹבָה:

| וּפִי־ | but mouth |
| אֱוִיל | foolish |
| מְחִתָּה | ruin/terror |
| קְרֹבָה | near/nearby |

---

A malevolent man's way is warped,
but a conscientious one conducts himself correctly.

PROV 21:8 ▪ DAY 224

## מִרְמָה בְּלֶב־חֹרְשֵׁי רָע

מִרְמָה   *deceit/treachery*

בְּלֶב־חֹרְשֵׁי   *in heart/mind of*
*ones who devise/plot/plan*

Qal Ptcp mp חרשׁ

רָע   *evil/harm/trouble*

## וּלְיֹעֲצֵי שָׁלוֹם שִׂמְחָה:

וּלְיֹעֲצֵי   *but for ones who counsel/advise*

Qal Ptcp mp יעץ + prep לְ + conj וְ

שָׁלוֹם   *peace/harmony/goodwill/friendship*

שִׂמְחָה   *joy/gladness/happiness/pleasure/mirth*

---

A conscientious man is cautious and eschews evil,
but a fool is full of fulminations, and he falls.

PROV 14:16 ▪ DAY 225

מְכַסֶּה שִׂנְאָה שִׂפְתֵי־שָׁקֶר

מְכַסֶּה    *one who conceals/covers up*

     Piel Ptcp ms כסה

שִׂנְאָה    *hatred/enmity*

שִׂפְתֵי־שָׁקֶר    *lips of*
        *falsehood/deceit/untruth/fraudulence*

וּמוֹצִא דִבָּה הוּא כְסִיל:

וּמוֹצִא    *and one who brings out*

     Hiph Ptcp ms יצא + conj וְ

דִבָּה    *slander/rumor/gossip*

הוּא    *he/that one*

כְסִיל    *fool/dolt/idiot*

---

Sages store up erudition;
but when an inept mouth is present, ruin is nigh.

PROV 10:14 ▪ DAY 226

יַסֵּר בִּנְךָ כִּי־יֵשׁ תִּקְוָה

| | |
|---|---|
| יַסֵּר | *instruct/train/educate/discipline/ correct/chastise/warn* |
| | Piel Impv ms יסר |
| בִּנְךָ | *your son/child* |
| כִּי־ | *for/because/while* |
| יֵשׁ | *there is* |
| תִּקְוָה | *hope* |

וְאֶל־הֲמִיתוֹ אַל־תִּשָּׂא נַפְשֶׁךָ:

| | |
|---|---|
| וְאֶל־הֲמִיתוֹ | *and/but toward causing him to die/ putting him to death* |
| | Hiph Inf Cst מות + 3ms sx |
| אַל־תִּשָּׂא | *do not lift up/raise* |
| | Qal Impf 2ms נשׂא |
| נַפְשֶׁךָ | *your soul/desire* |

---

Treachery is in the heart of renegades,
but there's gladness for those who encourage amity.

PROV 12:20 • DAY 227

עָרֵב לָאִישׁ לֶחֶם שָׁקֶר

| | |
|---|---|
| עָרֵב | *sweet/pleasant* |
| לָאִישׁ | *to the man/person* |
| לֶחֶם שָׁקֶר | *bread/food of*<br>*falsehood/deceit/untruth/fraudulence* |

וְאַחַר יִמָּלֵא־פִיהוּ חָצָץ׃

| | |
|---|---|
| וְאַחַר | *but afterward* |
| יִמָּלֵא־ | *(it) is filled*<br>Niph Impf 3ms מלא |
| פִיהוּ | *his mouth* |
| חָצָץ | *gravel* |

---

A man of duplicitous lips hides hatred,
and one who goes around gossiping—what a dolt!

PROV 10:18 ▪ DAY 228

מַלְאָךְ רָשָׁע יִפֹּל בְּרָע

| מַלְאָךְ | *messenger* |

| רָשָׁע | *wicked* |

| יִפֹּל | *(he) falls* |
| | נפל Qal Impf 3ms |

| בְּרָע | *into evil/trouble/calamity* |

וְצִיר אֱמוּנִים מַרְפֵּא:

| וְצִיר אֱמוּנִים | *but envoy of faithfulnesses/honesties* |

| מַרְפֵּא | *gentleness/calmness/healing* |

---

Discipline your child while there's hope,
but don't set your desire on causing his demise.

PROV 19:18 ▪ DAY 229

כָּבוֹד לָאִישׁ שֶׁבֶת מֵרִיב

| כָּבוֹד | honor/respect/reputation/glory |
|---|---|
| לָאִישׁ | for the man/person |
| שֶׁבֶת | cessation/desisting/refraining |
| מֵרִיב | from strife/dispute/quarrel/argument/lawsuit |

וְכָל־אֱוִיל יִתְגַּלָּע:

| וְכָל־אֱוִיל | but every fool |
|---|---|
| יִתְגַּלָּע | (he) breaks out/bursts out |
| | Hith Impf 3ms גלע |

---

Swindled bread is sweet to a man,
but afterward his mouth is full of gravel.

PROV 20:17 ▪ DAY 230

# פָּגוֹשׁ דֹּב שַׁכּוּל בְּאִישׁ

| פָּגוֹשׁ | *meeting/encountering* |
|---|---|
| | Qal Inf Abs פגשׁ |
| דֹּב | *bear* |
| שַׁכּוּל | *bereaved/deprived* |
| בְּאִישׁ | *(with) man/person* |

# וְאַל־כְּסִיל בְּאִוַּלְתּוֹ:

| וְאַל־ | *but not* |
|---|---|
| כְּסִיל | *fool/dolt/idiot* |
| בְּאִוַּלְתּוֹ | *in his folly* |

---

An evil envoy falls into trouble,
but an honest emissary is a remedy.

PROV 13:17 ▪ DAY 231

# בְּיִרְאַת יֱהֹוָה מִבְטַח־עֹז

| | |
|---:|:---|
| בְּיִרְאַת יֱהֹוָה | *in/through fear/awe/reverence of* **YHWH** |
| מִבְטַח־עֹז | *confidence/trust of strength* |

# וּלְבָנָיו יִהְיֶה מַחְסֶה:

| | |
|---:|:---|
| וּלְבָנָיו | *and for his children* |
| יִהְיֶה | *he/there will be* היה Qal Impf 3ms |
| מַחְסֶה | *refuge/shelter* |

---

There's respect for one who drops a dispute,
but every fool fulminates.

PROV 20:3 ▪ DAY 232

## תּוֹחֶלֶת מְמֻשָּׁכָה מַחֲלָה־לֵֽב

| תּוֹחֶלֶת | hope/expectation |
|---|---|
| מְמֻשָּׁכָה | (one that is) drawn out/prolonged/ delayed |
| | Pual Ptcp fs משׁך |
| מַחֲלָה־ | (it) makes sick |
| | Hiph Ptcp fs חלה |
| לֵב | heart/mind |

## וְעֵץ חַיִּים תַּאֲוָה בָאָֽה:

| וְעֵץ חַיִּים | but tree of life |
|---|---|
| תַּאֲוָה | desire/longing |
| בָאָה | (one) that arrives |
| | Qal Ptcp fs בוא |

---

Better to meet a bereaved bear
than a boor on a bender.

PROV 17:12 • DAY 233

מֹאזְנֵי מִרְמָה תּוֹעֲבַת יְהוָה

מֹאזְנֵי מִרְמָה    *scales/balances of deceit/treachery*

תּוֹעֲבַת יְהוָה    *abomination of* **YHWH**

וְאֶבֶן שְׁלֵמָה רְצוֹנוֹ:

וְאֶבֶן    *but stone/weight*

שְׁלֵמָה    *complete/proper*

רְצוֹנוֹ    *his delight/desire/favor*

---

There's robust strength in revering YHWH,
and one's descendants will have a refuge.

PROV 14:26 ▪ DAY 234

עֵקֶב עֲנָוָה יִרְאַת יְהוָה

| עֵקֶב עֲנָוָה | result/consequence of humility/meekness |
| יִרְאַת יְהוָה | fear/awe/reverence of **YHWH** |

עֹשֶׁר וְכָבוֹד וְחַיִּים:

| עֹשֶׁר | wealth |
| וְכָבוֹד | and honor/respect/reputation/glory |
| וְחַיִּים | and life |

---

Delayed expectation makes the heart ill,
but a longing fulfilled is a tree of life.

PROV 13:12 ▪ DAY 235

## אַל־תֹּאמַר אֲשַׁלְּמָה־רָע

אַל־תֹּאמַר    *do not say*

       Qal Impf 2ms אמר

אֲשַׁלְּמָה־    *let me repay/requite*

       Piel Coh 1cs שלם

רָע    *evil/harm*

## קַוֵּה לַיהוָֹה וְיֹשַׁע לָךְ׃

קַוֵּה    *wait*

       Piel Impv ms קוה

לַיהוָֹה    *for* YHWH

וְיֹשַׁע    *and let him save/deliver/rescue*

       Hiph Juss 3ms ישע + conj וְ

לָךְ    *you*

---

Skewed balances are abominable to YHWH,
but a sound stone is his desire.

PROV 11:1 ▪ DAY 236

שֵׂכֶל־טוֹב יִתֶּן־חֵן

| שֵׂכֶל־ | *prudence/wisdom/understanding* |
|---|---|
| טוֹב | *good* |
| יִתֶּן־ | *(it) gives/produces* <br> נתן Qal Impf 3ms |
| חֵן | *favor/grace/elegance* |

וְדֶרֶךְ בֹּגְדִים אֵיתָן׃

| וְדֶרֶךְ בֹּגְדִים | *but way/path of* <br> *ones who are treacherous* <br> בגד Qal Ptcp mp |
|---|---|
| אֵיתָן | *constant/enduring/permanent* |

---

The result of self-mortification and reverence for YHWH is
riches, reputation, and life.

PROV 22:4 ▪ DAY 237

יָד לְיָד לֹא־יִנָּקֶה רָע

| | |
|---|---|
| יָד | *hand* |
| לְיָד | *to hand* |
| לֹא־יִנָּקֶה | *(he) will not go unpunished* |
| | נקה Niph Impf 3ms |
| רָע | *evil/bad person* |

וְזֶרַע צַדִּיקִים נִמְלָט:

| | |
|---|---|
| וְזֶרַע צַדִּיקִים | *but seed/offspring of righteous people* |
| נִמְלָט | *(one that) escapes // (it) escapes* |
| | מלט Niph Ptcp ms |
| | מלט Niph Pf 3ms |

---

Don't say, "I'll get payback for harm!"
Wait for YHWH, and allow him to deliver you.

PROV 20:22 ▪ DAY 238

בְּאֹרַח־צְדָקָה חַיִּים

| | |
|---|---|
| בְּאֹרַח־צְדָקָה | *in/through way/path of righteousness/truthfulness/justice* |
| חַיִּים | *life* |

וְדֶרֶךְ נְתִיבָה אַל־מָוֶת:

| | |
|---|---|
| וְדֶרֶךְ | *and way/path* |
| נְתִיבָה | *path* |
| אַל־ | *not* |
| מָוֶת | *death* |

Good prudence produces favor,
but the way of the wanton is unwavering.

PROV 13:15 • DAY 239

אִישׁ בְּלִיַּעַל כֹּרֶה רָעָה

| אִישׁ בְּלִיַּעַל | *man/person of worthlessness/wickedness* |
| כֹּרֶה | *(one who) digs* |
| | Qal Ptcp ms כרה |
| רָעָה | *evil/harm/trouble/calamity/disaster* |

וְעַל־שְׂפָתוֹ כְּאֵשׁ צָרָבֶת׃

| וְעַל־שְׂפָתוֹ | *and on his lip* |
| | וְעַל־שׂפתיו KETIV |
| כְּאֵשׁ | *like fire* |
| צָרָבֶת | *scorching* |

> Assuredly, a wayward man won't get away with it;
> but the offspring of the upright escapes.
>
> PROV 11:21 ▪ DAY 240

# בְּבוֹא־רָשָׁע בָּא גַם־בּוּז

בְּבוֹא־רָשָׁע    *in/through/with coming of wicked person*

Qal Inf Cst בוא + prep בְּ

בָּא    *(it) comes*

Qal Pf 3ms בוא

גַם־    *also*

בּוּז    *contempt*

# וְעִם־קָלוֹן חֶרְפָּה׃

וְעִם־קָלוֹן    *and with shame/dishonor/disgrace*

חֶרְפָּה    *reproach/disgrace/scorn*

---

Life is on the righteous road;
indeed, it's a path, a peregrination, that doesn't lead to death.

PROV 12:28 ▪ DAY 241

קֶסֶם ׀ עַל־שִׂפְתֵי־מֶלֶךְ

| | |
|---|---|
| קֶסֶם ׀ | *omen/divination* |
| עַל־שִׂפְתֵי־מֶלֶךְ | *on lips of king/ruler* |

בְּמִשְׁפָּט לֹא יִמְעַל־פִּיו:

| | |
|---|---|
| בְּמִשְׁפָּט | *in judgment* |
| לֹא יִמְעַל־ | *(it) does not act unfaithfully/ treacherously* |
| | Qal Impf 3ms מעל |
| פִּיו | *his mouth* |

---

A scoundrel digs for disaster,
and on his lips it's like scorching fire.

PROV 16:27 ▪ DAY 242

# אִוֶּלֶת קְשׁוּרָה בְלֶב־נָעַר

| אִוֶּלֶת | *folly* |
|---|---|
| קְשׁוּרָה | *(that which) is bound up/plotted/ conspired* |

Qal Pass Ptcp fs קשר

| בְלֶב־נָעַר | *in heart/mind of young person/child* |
|---|---|

# שֵׁבֶט מוּסָר יַרְחִיקֶנָּה מִמֶּנּוּ׃

| שֵׁבֶט מוּסָר | *rod of chastisement/discipline/correction/ instruction* |
|---|---|
| יַרְחִיקֶנָּה | *(it) will keep/drive it far* |

Hiph Impf 3ms רחק + 3fs sx

| מִמֶּנּוּ | *from him* |
|---|---|

---

When a cantankerous man comes, contempt does too—
and with shame, scorn.

PROV 18:3 ▪ DAY 243

הֲלוֹא־יִתְעוּ חֹרְשֵׁי רָע

| הֲלוֹא־יִתְעוּ | *do (they) not go astray?* |
| | Qal Impf 3mp תעה |
| חֹרְשֵׁי | *ones who devise/plot/plan* |
| | Qal Ptcp mp חרשׁ |
| רָע | *evil/harm/trouble* |

וְחֶסֶד וֶאֱמֶת חֹרְשֵׁי טוֹב:

| וְחֶסֶד | *but lovingkindness/faithfulness/loyalty/ steadfast love/probity* |
| וֶאֱמֶת | *and truth/honesty/trustworthiness/ faithfulness* |
| חֹרְשֵׁי | *ones who devise/plan* |
| | Qal Ptcp mp חרשׁ |
| טוֹב | *good/goodness/benefit* |

---

Prescience is on a potentate's lips;
when arbitrating, his mouth is not arbitrary.

PROV 16:10 ▪ DAY 244

## גָּמֵל נַפְשׁוֹ אִישׁ חֶסֶד

גָּמֵל — (one who) does good to/rewards/deals with

Qal Ptcp ms גמל

נַפְשׁוֹ — his soul/self

אִישׁ חֶסֶד — man/person of lovingkindness/faithfulness/loyalty/ steadfast love/probity

## וְעֹכֵר שְׁאֵרוֹ אַכְזָרִי׃

וְעֹכֵר — but one who troubles

Qal Ptcp ms עבר + conj וְ

שְׁאֵרוֹ — his body/self/kin

אַכְזָרִי — cruel/merciless

---

Irrationality is bound up in a young man's heart;
a chastening rod will drive it far from him.

PROV 22:15  •  DAY 245

אוֹצָר | נֶחְמָד וָשֶׁמֶן בִּנְוֵה חָכָם

| | |
|---|---|
| אוֹצָר | *treasure* |
| נֶחְמָד | *(that which is) desirable/pleasing*<br>Niph Ptcp ms חמד |
| וָשֶׁמֶן | *and oil* |
| בִּנְוֵה חָכָם | *in dwelling of*<br>*wise/sage person* |

וּכְסִיל אָדָם יְבַלְּעֶנּוּ׃

| | |
|---|---|
| וּכְסִיל אָדָם | *but fool/dolt of*<br>*man/person* |
| יְבַלְּעֶנּוּ | *(he) devours it/swallows it up*<br>Piel Impf 3ms בלע + 3ms sx |

---

Do not conspirators go astray?
But trustworthiness and truth are with those whose plans are beneficial.

PROV 14:22 ▪ DAY 246

שֹׁחֵר ֯טוֹב יְבַקֵּשׁ רָצֹון

| | |
|---:|:---|
| שֹׁחֵר | *one who seeks* |
| | Qal Ptcp ms שׁחר |
| ֯טוֹב | *good/goodness/benefit* |
| יְבַקֵּשׁ | *(he) seeks* |
| | Piel Impf 3ms בקשׁ |
| רָצֹון | *favor/delight* |

וְדֹרֵשׁ רָעָה תְבֹואֶנּוּ׃

| | |
|---:|:---|
| וְדֹרֵשׁ | *but one who seeks* |
| | Qal Ptcp ms דרשׁ + conj וְ |
| רָעָה | *evil/harm/trouble/calamity/disaster* |
| תְבֹואֶנּוּ | *it will come to/upon him* |
| | Qal Impf 3fs בוא + 3ms sx |

---

A steadfast man takes care of himself,
but one who troubles his body is cruel.

PROV 11:17 ▪ DAY 247

בֵּית רְשָׁעִים יִשָּׁמֵד

| | |
|---|---|
| בֵּית רְשָׁעִים | *house/household/home/family/dynasty of wicked/guilty people* |
| יִשָּׁמֵד | *(it) will be destroyed/wiped out* |
| | Niph Impf 3ms שמד |

וְאֹהֶל יְשָׁרִים יַפְרִיחַ:

| | |
|---|---|
| וְאֹהֶל יְשָׁרִים | *but tent of upright people* |
| יַפְרִיחַ | *(it) will flourish* |
| | Hiph Impf 3ms פרח |

---

Cherished treasure and oil are in an astute man's abode,
but a dolt of a man devours them.

PROV 21:20 ▪ DAY 248

# גַּם־בִּשְׂחֹוק יִכְאַב־לֵב

| | |
|---|---|
| גַּם־ | *even* |
| בִּשְׂחֹוק | *in laughing/pleasure* |
| יִכְאַב־ | *(it) may ache/be in pain* |
| | Qal Impf 3ms כאב |
| לֵב | *heart/mind/conscience* |

# וְאַחֲרִיתָהּ שִׂמְחָה תוּגָה:

| | |
|---|---|
| וְאַחֲרִיתָהּ | *and its end/future* |
| שִׂמְחָה | *joy/gladness/happiness/pleasure/mirth* |
| תוּגָה | *grief/sorrow* |

---

One who seeks excellence searches for favor,
but he who asks for trouble—it will find him.

PROV 11:27 ▪ DAY 249

לֹא־נָאוָה לְנָבָל שְׂפַת־יֶתֶר

לֹא־          *not*

נָאוָה        *fitting/suitable*

לְנָבָל       *for foolish/ignominious/godless/*
            *worthless person*

שְׂפַת־יֶתֶר   *lip of*
            *excess/abundance/excellence/*
            *preeminence*

אַף כִּי־לְנָדִיב שְׂפַת־שָׁקֶר:

אַף כִּי־      *how much less*

לְנָדִיב       *for generous person/noble*

שְׂפַת־שָׁקֶר   *lip of*
            *falsehood/deceit/untruth/fraudulence*

---

The house of the wicked will be wiped out,
but the tent of the upright will thrive.

PROV 14:11 ▪ DAY 250

# צַדִּיק הָרִאשׁוֹן בְּרִיבוֹ

| צַדִּיק | *righteous/right/correct* |
| --- | --- |
| הָרִאשׁוֹן | *the first person* |
| בְּרִיבוֹ | *in his lawsuit/legal case/dispute/ argument/quarrel* |

# וּבָא־רֵעֵהוּ וַחֲקָרוֹ:

| וּבָא־ | *then (he) comes* |
| --- | --- |
| | Qal weqatal 3ms בוא |
| | KETIV ‏יבא־ |
| רֵעֵהוּ | *his neighbor* |
| וַחֲקָרוֹ | *and/then (he) examines/ investigates him/it* |
| | Qal weqatal 3ms חקר + 3ms sx |

---

Even when guffawing one's heart may ache,
and gladness can give way to grief.

PROV 14:13 ▪ DAY 251

## חַכְמוֹת נָשִׁים בָּנְתָה בֵיתָהּ

| | |
|---|---|
| חַכְמוֹת נָשִׁים | *wise woman of women* |
| בָּנְתָה | *(she) builds/constructs* |
| | בנה Qal Pf 3fs |
| בֵיתָהּ | *her house/household/home/family/ dynasty* |

## וְאִוֶּלֶת בְּיָדֶיהָ תֶהֶרְסֶנּוּ׃

| | |
|---|---|
| וְאִוֶּלֶת | *but folly* |
| בְּיָדֶיהָ | *with her hands* |
| תֶהֶרְסֶנּוּ | *(she/it) tears it down* |
| | Qal Impf 3fs הרס + 3ms sx |

---

It's not appropriate for a depraved man to palaver,
how much less for a noble to have lying lips!

PROV 17:7 ▪ DAY 252

אֶבֶן־חֵן הַשֹּׁחַד בְּעֵינֵי בְעָלָיו

| | |
|---|---|
| אֶבֶן־חֵן | *stone of charm/elegance* |
| הַשֹּׁחַד | *the bribe* |
| בְּעֵינֵי בְעָלָיו | *in eyes of its possessor/owner* |

אֶל־כָּל־אֲשֶׁר יִפְנֶה יַשְׂכִּיל:

| | |
|---|---|
| אֶל־כָּל־אֲשֶׁר יִפְנֶה | *to/toward all that he turns* <br> פנה Qal Impf 3ms |
| יַשְׂכִּיל | *he succeeds* <br> שׂכל Hiph Impf 3ms |

---

The first person in a lawsuit appears correct,
but then someone comes and cross-examines him.

PROV 18:17 ▪ DAY 253

טָמַן עָצֵל יָדוֹ בַּצַּלָּחַת

| | |
|---|---|
| טָמַן | (he) buries/hides/conceals |
| | Qal Pf 3ms טמן |
| עָצֵל | lazy/sluggish/slothful person |
| יָדוֹ | his hand |
| בַּצַּלָּחַת | in the dish |

גַּם־אֶל־פִּיהוּ לֹא יְשִׁיבֶנָּה׃

| | |
|---|---|
| גַּם־ | yet/even |
| אֶל־פִּיהוּ | to/toward his mouth |
| לֹא יְשִׁיבֶנָּה | he does not bring it back |
| | Hiph Impf 3ms שׁוב + 3fs sx |

---

A wholly wise woman constructs her house,
but folly tears it down with her hands.

PROV 14:1 ▪ DAY 254

צִנִּ֤ים פַּחִים֮ בְּדֶ֪רֶךְ עִקֵּ֥שׁ

| | |
|---|---|
| צִנִּ֤ים | *thorns* |
| פַּחִים֮ | *snares/traps* |
| בְּדֶ֪רֶךְ | *in/on way/path* |
| עִקֵּ֥שׁ | *perverse/crooked/twisted* |

שׁוֹמֵ֥ר נַ֝פְשׁ֗וֹ יִרְחַ֥ק מֵהֶֽם׃

| | |
|---|---|
| שׁוֹמֵ֥ר | *one who guards/keeps/preserves/ protects* |
| | Qal Ptcp ms שמר |
| נַ֝פְשׁ֗וֹ | *his soul/life/self* |
| יִרְחַ֥ק | *(he) will be far/distant* |
| | Qal Impf 3ms רחק |
| מֵהֶֽם | *from them* |

---

A bribe is a precious stone in its possessor's eyes;
he succeeds wheresoever he turns.

PROV 17:8 ▪ DAY 255

חַיֵּי בְשָׂרִים לֵב מַרְפֵּא

| חַיֵּי בְשָׂרִים | *life of* |
| | *bodies* |

| לֵב מַרְפֵּא | *heart/mind of* |
| | *gentleness/calmness/healing* |

וּרְקַב עֲצָמוֹת קִנְאָה׃

| וּרְקַב עֲצָמוֹת | *but rot/decay of* |
| | *bones* |

| קִנְאָה | *passion/jealousy/envy* |

---

A slothful man sinks his hand in the dish;
he can't even bring it back to his mouth.

PROV 19:24 ▪ DAY 256

## הַוֺּת לְאָבִיו בֵּן כְּסִיל

| | |
|---|---|
| הַוֺּת | ruinations/destructions/mischiefs |
| לְאָבִיו | to his father/parent |
| בֵּן | son/child |
| כְּסִיל | foolish/stupid |

## וְדֶלֶף טֹרֵד מִדְיְנֵי אִשָּׁה׃

| | |
|---|---|
| וְדֶלֶף | and dripping/leaking |
| טֹרֵד | (that which is) continual<br>Qal Ptcp ms טרד |
| מִדְיְנֵי אִשָּׁה | quarrels/contentions of woman/wife |

---

Thorns and traps are on the perverse path;
he who prizes self-preservation keeps far from them.

PROV 22:5 ▪ DAY 257

אִישׁ חֵמָה יְגָרֶה מָדוֹן

| | |
|---|---|
| אִישׁ חֵמָה | *man of wrath/anger/fury* |
| יְגָרֶה | *(he) stirs up/provokes/engages in* <br> Piel Impf 3ms גרה |
| מָדוֹן | *strife/contention* |

וְאֶרֶךְ אַפַּיִם יַשְׁקִיט רִיב:

| | |
|---|---|
| וְאֶרֶךְ אַפַּיִם | *but one long of [i.e., slow to] anger* |
| יַשְׁקִיט | *(he) quiets/calms* <br> Hiph Impf 3ms שקט |
| רִיב | *strife/dispute/quarrel/argument* |

---

Calm mind, healthy body—
but jealousy is rot to the bones.

PROV 14:30 ▪ DAY 258

# תּוֹרַת חָכָם מְקוֹר חַיִּים

| | |
|---|---|
| תּוֹרַת חָכָם | *teaching/instruction of wise/sage person* |
| מְקוֹר חַיִּים | *fountain/spring/source of life* |

# לָסוּר מִמֹּקְשֵׁי מָוֶת׃

| | |
|---|---|
| לָסוּר | *to turn away/aside* |
| | Qal Inf Cst סוּר + prep לְ |
| מִמֹּקְשֵׁי מָוֶת | *from snares/traps/baits of death* |

---

A stupid kid is his dad's destruction,
and a wife's squabbles are a nonstop drip.

PROV 19:13 ▪ DAY 259

קְנֹה־חָכְמָה מַה־טּוֹב מֵחָרוּץ

| | |
|---|---|
| קְנֹה־ | *to acquire/get/gain/obtain*<br>Qal Inf Cst קנה |
| חָכְמָה | *wisdom* |
| מַה־ | *how much* |
| טּוֹב | *better* |
| מֵחָרוּץ | *than gold* |

וּקְנוֹת בִּינָה נִבְחָר מִכָּסֶף:

| | |
|---|---|
| וּקְנוֹת | *and to acquire/get/gain/obtain*<br>וְ conj + קנה Qal Inf Cst |
| בִּינָה | *understanding/discernment* |
| נִבְחָר | *(it) is preferable*<br>Niph Ptcp ms בחר |
| מִכָּסֶף | *to/more than/instead of silver* |

---

A hothead stirs up strife,
but a cool-tempered person calms a quarrel.

PROV 15:18 ▪ DAY 260

גֹּל אֶל־יְהוָה מַעֲשֶׂיךָ

| | |
|---|---|
| גֹּל | *roll* |
| | גלל Qal Impv ms |
| אֶל־יְהוָה | *to/toward YHWH* |
| מַעֲשֶׂיךָ | *your deeds/works* |

וְיִכֹּנוּ מַחְשְׁבֹתֶיךָ׃

| | |
|---|---|
| וְיִכֹּנוּ | *and (they) will be established/secure/ready* |
| | כון Niph Impf 3mp + conj וְ |
| מַחְשְׁבֹתֶיךָ | *your thoughts/plans* |

---

A sage's training is a spring of life,
turning one away from deadly bait.

PROV 13:14 ▪ DAY 261

## עֵד־כְּזָבִים יֹאבֵד

עֵד־כְּזָבִים    *witness/testimony of lies/falsehoods*

יֹאבֵד    *(he/it) will perish/be destroyed*
Qal Impf 3ms אבד

## וְאִישׁ שׁוֹמֵעַ לָנֶצַח יְדַבֵּר׃

וְאִישׁ    *but man/person*

שׁוֹמֵעַ    *(one) who hears/listens*
Qal Ptcp ms שׁמע

לָנֶצַח    *forever/for glory/to victory*

יְדַבֵּר    *(he) will speak // (he) will have descendants*
Piel Impf 3ms דבר

---

Far better to gain enlightenment than gold,
and developing discernment is choicer than silver.

PROV 16:16 ▪ DAY 262

# בּוֹטֵחַ בְּעָשְׁרוֹ הוּא יִפֹּל

| | |
|---|---|
| בּוֹטֵחַ | *one who trusts/is confident/is secure/ [falls]* |
| | Qal Ptcp ms בטח |
| בְּעָשְׁרוֹ | *in his wealth* |
| הוּא | *he/that one* |
| יִפֹּל | *(he) will fall* |
| | Qal Impf 3ms נפל |

# וְכֶעָלֶה צַדִּיקִים יִפְרָחוּ׃

| | |
|---|---|
| וְכֶעָלֶה | *but like the leaf* |
| צַדִּיקִים | *righteous people* |
| יִפְרָחוּ | *(they) will flourish* |
| | Qal Impf 3mp פרח |

---

Roll your activities toward YHWH,
and your plans will prosper.

PROV 16:3  ▪  DAY 263

נֶ֤פֶשׁ עָמֵ֣ל עָֽמְלָה־לּ֑וֹ

| | |
|---|---|
| נֶ֤פֶשׁ עָמֵ֣ל | *throat/appetite/desire of worker/toiler* |
| עָֽמְלָה | *(it) works/toils* |
| | Qal Pf 3fs עמל |
| לּ֑וֹ | *for him* |

כִּֽי־אָכַ֖ף עָלָ֣יו פִּֽיהוּ׃

| | |
|---|---|
| כִּֽי־ | *for/because/indeed* |
| אָכַ֖ף | *(it) presses* |
| | Qal Pf 3ms אכף |
| עָלָ֣יו | *upon him* |
| פִּֽיהוּ | *his mouth* |

---

Truthless testimony will perish,
but a person who listens will speak prevailingly.

PROV 21:28 ▪ DAY 264

יֵשׁ זָהָב וְרַב־פְּנִינִים

יֵשׁ　　there is

זָהָב　　gold

וְרַב־פְּנִינִים　　and abundance/multitude of
　　　　　　　jewels

וּכְלִי יְקָר שִׂפְתֵי־דָעַת׃

וּכְלִי יְקָר　　and/but object/article/tool of
　　　　　　preciousness

שִׂפְתֵי־דָעַת　　lips of
　　　　　　knowledge

---

One who trusts in his assets will certainly fall,
but the righteous will flourish like a leaf.

PROV 11:28 ▪ DAY 265

עֹבֵד אַדְמָתוֹ יִשְׂבַּע־לָחֶם

עֹבֵד    *one who works*
    Qal Ptcp ms עבד

אַדְמָתוֹ    *his ground/earth*

יִשְׂבַּע־    *(he) will be satisfied/satiated/full*
    Qal Impf 3ms שבע

לָחֶם    *bread/food*

וּמְרַדֵּף רֵיקִים חֲסַר־לֵב:

וּמְרַדֵּף    *but one who pursues*
    Piel Ptcp ms רדף + conj וְ

רֵיקִים    *empty things*

חֲסַר־לֵב    *lacking/devoid of
    heart/mind/understanding/
    conscience*

---

A laborer's appetite toils for him;
indeed, his palate urges him on.

PROV 16:26 ▪ DAY 266

סוּס מוּכָן לְיוֹם מִלְחָמָה

| | |
|---|---|
| סוּס | *horse* |
| מוּכָן | *(one that) is made ready/prepared* |
| | כון Hoph Ptcp ms |
| לְיוֹם מִלְחָמָה | *for day of battle/war* |

וְלַיהוָֹה הַתְּשׁוּעָה׃

| | |
|---|---|
| וְלַיהוָֹה | *but to* YHWH |
| הַתְּשׁוּעָה | *the victory/deliverance/rescue* |

---

There's gold and a bevy of jewels,
but loquacious lips are a precious commodity.

PROV 20:15 ▪ DAY 267

# שְׂפַת־אֱמֶת תִּכּוֹן לָעַד

| | |
|---|---|
| שְׂפַת־אֱמֶת | *lip/speech of truth/honesty/trustworthiness/ faithfulness* |
| תִּכּוֹן | *(it) will be established/secure* <br> Niph Impf 3fs כּוּן |
| לָעַד | *for perpetuity/forever* |

# וְעַד־אַרְגִּיעָה לִשְׁוֹן שָׁקֶר:

| | |
|---|---|
| וְעַד־אַרְגִּיעָה | *but for moment* |
| לִשְׁוֹן שָׁקֶר | *tongue of falsehood/deceit/untruth/fraudulence* |

---

One who works his land will be filled with food,
but one who chases trifles lacks wits.

PROV 12:11 ▪ DAY 268

לְא־נָאוֶה לִכְסִיל תַּעֲנֻוג

| | |
|---|---|
| לֹא־ | *not* |
| נָאוֶה | *fitting/suitable* |
| לִכְסִיל | *for fool/dolt/idiot* |
| תַּעֲנֻוג | *luxury* |

אַף כִּי־לְעֶבֶד‌ מְשֹׁל בְּשָׂרִים׃

| | |
|---|---|
| אַף כִּי־ | *how much less* |
| לְעֶבֶד‌ | *for slave/servant* |
| מְשֹׁל | *to rule* |
| | Qal Inf Cst מְשֹׁל |
| בְּשָׂרִים | *over princes/leaders/officials* |

---

A steed is groomed for the day of battle,
but the triumph belongs to YHWH.

PROV 21:31 ▪ DAY 269

עֹצֶה עֵינָיו לַחְשֹׁב תַּהְפֻּכוֹת

| | |
|---|---|
| עֹצֶה | *one who winks* |
| | Qal Ptcp ms עצה |
| עֵינָיו | *his eyes* |
| לַחְשֹׁב | *to plan* |
| | לְ prep + חשׁב Qal Inf Cst |
| תַּהְפֻּכוֹת | *perversities* |

קֹרֵץ שְׂפָתָיו כִּלָּה רָעָה׃

| | |
|---|---|
| קֹרֵץ | *one who pinches/compresses* |
| | Qal Ptcp ms קרץ |
| שְׂפָתָיו | *his lips* |
| כִּלָּה | *(he) brings to completion* |
| | Piel Pf 3ms כלה |
| רָעָה | *evil/harm/trouble/calamity/disaster* |

---

Sincere speech is secure forever,
but a lying tongue, only for a second.

PROV 12:19 ▪ DAY 270

מֵרַע מַקְשִׁיב עַל־שְׂפַת־אָֽוֶן

| | |
|---|---|
| מֵרַע | one who does evil/wrong |
| | Hiph Ptcp ms רעע |
| מַקְשִׁיב | one who pays attention |
| | Hiph Ptcp ms קשׁב |
| עַל־שְׂפַת־אָֽוֶן | to lip/speech of iniquity/injustice/sin/evil |

שֶׁקֶר מֵזִין עַל־לְשׁוֹן הַוֹּֽת׃

| | |
|---|---|
| שֶׁקֶר | falsehood/deceit/lie/untruth/ fraudulence |
| מֵזִין | one who inclines ear |
| | Hiph Ptcp ms אזן |
| עַל־לְשׁוֹן הַוֹּֽת | to tongue of malices/mischiefs |

---

Opulence isn't appropriate for an ignoramus,
how much less that a slave rule over princes!

PROV 19:10 ▪ DAY 271

# אָדָ֗ם תּ֭וֹעֶה מִדֶּ֣רֶךְ הַשְׂכֵּ֑ל

אָדָ֗ם *man/person*

תּ֭וֹעֶה *(one) who strays*
   Qal Ptcp ms תעה

מִדֶּ֣רֶךְ הַשְׂכֵּ֑ל *from way/path of*
   *prudence/wisdom/understanding*
   Hiph Inf Abs שׂכל

# בִּקְהַ֖ל רְפָאִ֣ים יָנֽוּחַ׃

בִּקְהַ֖ל רְפָאִ֣ים *in assembly/congregation of*
   *shades/dead spirits*

יָנֽוּחַ *(he) will rest*
   Qal Impf 3ms נוח

---

A conniver plans perversities;
one who curls his lips brings calamity to completion.

PROV 16:30 ▪ DAY 272

פֶּתִי יַאֲמִין לְכָל־דָּבָר

| פֶּתִי | simpleminded/naïve/ignorant person |
| יַאֲמִין | (he) believes/trusts |
| | Hiph Impf 3ms אמן |
| לְכָל־דָּבָר | every word/statement // everything |

וְעָרוּם יָבִין לַאֲשֻׁרוֹ׃

| וְעָרוּם | but prudent/shrewd/clever person |
| יָבִין | (he) understands/discerns/perceives |
| | Qal Impf 3ms בין |
| לַאֲשֻׁרוֹ | his step/path/course |

---

One who gives credence to libelous lips does evil;
one who inclines his ear to a malicious tongue is a lie.

PROV 17:4 ▪ DAY 273

# בֵּית גֵּאִים יִסַּח ׀ יְהוָה

| | |
|---:|:---|
| בֵּית גֵּאִים | *house/household/home/family/dynasty of haughty/proud people* |
| יִסַּח ׀ | *(he) tears down/uproots* <br> נסח Qal Impf 3ms |
| יְהוָה | *YHWH* |

# וְיַצֵּב גְּבוּל אַלְמָנָה:

| | |
|---:|:---|
| וְיַצֵּב | *(but) he establishes* <br> וְ + נצב Hiph Impf 3ms + conj |
| גְּבוּל אַלְמָנָה | *boundary of* <br> *widow* |

---

A person who strays from the prudent path
will repose in the company of wraiths.

PROV 21:16 ▪ DAY 274

טֹוב שְׁפַל־רוּחַ אֶת־עֲנָוִים

| | |
|---|---|
| טֹוב | *better* |
| שְׁפַל־רוּחַ | *one humble of/one who is humble of/ to be humble of* <br> *spirit* <br> שָׁפָל adj <br> שׁפל Qal Ptcp ms <br> שׁפל Qal Inf Cst |
| אֶת־עֲנָוִים | *with lowly/afflicted/humble/dejected people* <br> KETIV אֶת־עניים |

מֵחַלֵּק שָׁלָל אֶת־גֵּאִים׃

| | |
|---|---|
| מֵחַלֵּק | *than to divide/share* <br> Piel Inf Cst חלק + prep מִן |
| שָׁלָל | *plunder/booty* |
| אֶת־גֵּאִים | *with haughty/proud people* |

---

An ignoramus will believe anything,
but a shrewd man understands his steps.

PROV 14:15 ▪ DAY 275

טֽוֹב לָשֶׁ֫בֶת עַל־פִּנַּת־גָּ֑ג

| | |
|---|---|
| טֽוֹב | *better* |
| לָשֶׁ֫בֶת | *to sit/live/dwell* |
| | לְ + prep + יָשַׁב Qal Inf Cst |
| עַל־פִּנַּת־גָּ֑ג | *on corner of*<br>*roof* |

מֵאֵ֥שֶׁת מִדְיָנִ֗ים וּבֵ֥ית חָ֥בֶר:

| | |
|---|---|
| מֵאֵ֥שֶׁת מִדְיָנִ֗ים | *than woman/wife of*<br>*quarrels/contentions* |
| וּבֵ֥ית חָ֥בֶר | *and house/home of*<br>*association/company* |

---

YHWH tears down the house of the haughty,
but he delimits a plot for the widow.

PROV 15:25 ▪ DAY 276

# רַע־יֵרֹועַ כִּי־עָ֣רַב זָ֑ר

רַע־     *evil/harm/calamity*

יֵרֹועַ     *he will suffer evil/harm/calamity*
        Niph Impf 3ms רעע

כִּי־     *when/for/because*

עָ֣רַב     *he has become/stood surety for*
        Qal Pf 3ms ערב

זָ֑ר     *stranger*

# וְשֹׂנֵא תֹקְעִים בֹּוטֵחַ:

וְשֹׂנֵא     *but one who hates*
        Qal Ptcp ms שׂנא + conj וְ

תֹקְעִים     *act of shaking hands in pledge*

בֹּוטֵחַ     *one who is secure/confident*
        Qal Ptcp ms בטח

---

Better to be lowly in spirit with outcasts
than to share plunder with the proud.

PROV 16:19 ▪ DAY 277

## טוֹב שֶׁבֶת בְּאֶרֶץ־מִדְבָּר

טוֹב     *better*

שֶׁבֶת     *to sit/live/dwell*
       Qal Inf Cst יָשַׁב

בְּאֶרֶץ־מִדְבָּר     *in land of desert/wilderness*

## מֵאֵשֶׁת מִדְיָנִים וָכָעַס:

מֵאֵשֶׁת מִדְיָנִים     *than woman/wife of quarrels/contentions*
       מֵאֵשֶׁת מדונים KETIV

וָכָעַס     *and vexation/anger/provocation*

---

Better to live on the corner of a roof
than in a shared space with a contentious spouse.

PROV 21:9 ▪ DAY 278

# רֽוּחַ־אִישׁ יְכַלְכֵּל מַחֲלֵהוּ

| | |
|---|---|
| רֽוּחַ־אִישׁ | *spirit of man/person* |
| יְכַלְכֵּל | *(it) endures* <br> Pilpel Impf 3ms כול |
| מַחֲלֵהוּ | *his sickness/disease* |

# וְרֽוּחַ נְכֵאָה מִי יִשָּׂאֶֽנָּה׃

| | |
|---|---|
| וְרֽוּחַ | *but spirit* |
| נְכֵאָה | *broken/crushed/stricken* |
| מִי | *who?* |
| יִשָּׂאֶֽנָּה | *(he) can bear/carry/raise it // (he) can lift it up* <br> Qal Impf 3ms נשׂא + 3fs sx |

---

He'll suffer harm, for he stood surety for a stranger;
but one who hates clasping hands in pledge is secure.

PROV 11:15 ▪ DAY 279

כַּעַס לְאָבִיו בֵּן כְּסִיל

| כַּעַס | *vexation/anger/provocation* |
| לְאָבִיו | *to his father* |
| בֵּן | *son/child* |
| כְּסִיל | *foolish/stupid* |

וּמֶמֶר לְיוֹלַדְתּוֹ:

| וּמֶמֶר | *and bitterness* |
| לְיוֹלַדְתּוֹ | *to one who bore him* |
|  | Qal Ptcp fs ילד + 3ms sx + prep לְ |

Better to dwell in a wasteland
than with a pugnacious and pugilistic spouse.

PROV 21:19 ▪ DAY 280

# דֶּרֶךְ עָצֵל כִּמְשֻׂכַת חָדֶק

| | |
|---|---|
| דֶּרֶךְ עָצֵל | *way/path of* |
| | *lazy/sluggish/slothful person* |
| כִּמְשֻׂכַת חָדֶק | *like hedge of* |
| | *briar* |

# וְאֹרַח יְשָׁרִים סְלֻלָה:

| | |
|---|---|
| וְאֹרַח יְשָׁרִים | *but way/path of* |
| | *upright people* |
| סְלֻלָה | *(one that) is built up/raised/paved* |
| | Qal Pass Ptcp fs סלל |

---

A person's spirit can endure a disease,
but who can sustain a scarred psyche?

PROV 18:14  ▪  DAY 281

בְּאוֹר־פְּנֵי־מֶלֶךְ חַיִּ֑ים

בְּאוֹר־פְּנֵי־מֶלֶךְ    *in light/shining of*
*face of*
*king/ruler*

בְּ prep + אוֹר noun

בְּ prep + אוֹר Qal Inf Cst

חַיִּ֑ים    *life*

וּרְצוֹנוֹ כְּעָב מַלְקוֹשׁ:

וּרְצוֹנוֹ    *and his favor/delight*

כְּעָב מַלְקוֹשׁ    *like cloud of*
*spring rain*

---

A senseless son is an irritant to his father
and bitterness to her who bore him.

PROV 17:25 ▪ DAY 282

## אֹהֵב מוּסָר אֹהֵב דָּעַת

אֹהֵב　　*one who loves*
　　　　Qal Ptcp ms אהב

מוּסָר　　*instruction/training/education/warning/discipline/correction/chastisement*

אֹהֵב　　*one who loves*
　　　　Qal Ptcp ms אהב

דָּעַת　　*knowledge*

## וְשֹׂנֵא תוֹכַחַת בָּעַר:

וְשֹׂנֵא　　*but one who hates*
　　　　Qal Ptcp ms שׂנא + conj וְ

תוֹכַחַת　　*reproof/rebuke*

בָּעַר　　*stupid/brutish*

---

A slothful person's path is like a thorny hedge,
but the way of the dependable is paved.

PROV 15:19　▪　DAY 283

מִי־יֹאמַר זִכִּיתִי לִבִּי

מִי־ *who?*

יֹאמַר *(he) can say*
אמר Qal Impf 3ms

זִכִּיתִי *I have made/kept pure*
זכה Piel Pf 1cs

לִבִּי *my heart/mind/conscience*

טָהַרְתִּי מֵחַטָּאתִי:

טָהַרְתִּי *I am clean/pure*
טהר Qal Pf 1cs

מֵחַטָּאתִי *from my sin*

---

There's life when a ruler's face shines,
and his favor is like a cloud of spring rain.

PROV 16:15 ▪ DAY 284

נֶ֫פֶשׁ־בְּרָכָ֥ה תְדֻשָּׁ֑ן

נֶ֫פֶשׁ־בְּרָכָ֥ה　*soul/person/life of blessing*

תְדֻשָּׁ֑ן　*(it) is fat/fattened // (it) will be made fat/fattened*
　　　　Pual Impf 3fs דשׁן

וּמַרְוֶ֗ה גַּם־ה֥וּא יוֹרֶֽא:

וּמַרְוֶ֗ה　*and one who waters/saturates*
　　　　Hiph Ptcp ms רוה + conj וְ

גַּם־　*also/likewise*

ה֥וּא　*he/that one*

יוֹרֶֽא　*(he) is watered/saturated // (he) will be watered/saturated // (he) will teach* (!)
　　　　Hoph Impf 3ms רוה

---

He who appreciates correction loves learning,
but he who hates rebuke is a brute.

PROV 12:1 ▪ DAY 285

טוֹב פַּת חֲרֵבָה וְשַׁלְוָה־בָהּ

| | |
|---|---|
| טוֹב | *better* |
| פַּת | *morsel* |
| חֲרֵבָה | *dry* |
| וְשַׁלְוָה־ | *and quiet/peace* |
| בָהּ | *with it* |

מִבַּיִת מָלֵא זִבְחֵי־רִיב:

| | |
|---|---|
| מִבַּיִת | *than house/household/home/family* |
| מָלֵא | *full* |
| זִבְחֵי־רִיב | *sacrifices of strife/dispute/quarrel/argument* |

---

Who can say, "I've maintained a pure heart,
I'm spotless from sin"?

PROV 20:9 ▪ DAY 286

## הוֹלֵ֤ךְ בַּתֹּם֙ יֵ֣לֶךְ בֶּ֑טַח

| | |
|---|---|
| הוֹלֵ֤ךְ | *one who walks* |
| | Qal Ptcp ms הלך |
| בַּתֹּם֙ | *in the integrity/innocence/blamelessness/ purity/perfection* |
| יֵ֣לֶךְ | *(he) walks* |
| | Qal Impf 3ms הלך |
| בֶּ֑טַח | *safety/security* |

## וּמְעַקֵּ֥שׁ דְּרָכָ֗יו יִוָּדֵֽעַ׃

| | |
|---|---|
| וּמְעַקֵּ֥שׁ | *but one who makes crooked/twists/ perverts* |
| | Piel Ptcp ms עקשׁ + conj וְ |
| דְּרָכָ֗יו | *his ways/paths* |
| יִוָּדֵֽעַ | *(he) makes himself known // (he) will be discovered* |
| | Niph Impf 3ms ידע |

---

A benevolent soul will become plump,
and one who waters will himself be drenched.

PROV 11:25 ▪ DAY 287

יִרְאַת יְהוָה לְחַיִּים

| | |
|---|---|
| יִרְאַת יְהוָה | *fear/awe/reverence of* **YHWH** |
| לְחַיִּים | *to/for life* |

וְשָׂבֵעַ יָלִין בַּל־יִפָּקֶד רָע׃

| | |
|---|---|
| וְשָׂבֵעַ | *and satisfied/satiated/full* |
| יָלִין | *he remains* <br> Qal Impf 3ms לין |
| בַּל־יִפָּקֶד | *he will not be visited* |
| רָע | *evil/harm/trouble/calamity/disaster* |

---

Better a brittle crust with quiet
than a house full of foods and feuds.

PROV 17:1 ▪ DAY 288

## טוֹב נִקְלֶה וְעֶבֶד לֽוֹ

| | |
|---:|:---|
| טוֹב | *better* |
| נִקְלֶה | *one who is lightly esteemed/insignificant* <br> Niph Ptcp ms קלה |
| וְעֶבֶד | *but servant/slave* |
| לֽוֹ | *to him* |

## מִמְּתַכַּבֵּד וַחֲסַר־לָֽחֶם:

| | |
|---:|:---|
| מִמְּתַכַּבֵּד | *than one who honors himself/considers himself important* <br> מִן prep + כבד Hith(!) Ptcp ms |
| וַחֲסַר־לָֽחֶם | *but lacking of bread/food* |

---

One whose deportment is flawless walks with assurance,
but one who perverts his paths will be found out.

PROV 10:9 ▪ DAY 289

אֱוִיל יִנְאַץ מוּסַר אָבִיו

אֱוִיל    *fool*

יִנְאַץ    *(he) spurns*
Qal Impf 3ms נאץ

מוּסַר אָבִיו    *instruction/training/education/warning/
discipline/correction/chastisement of
his father/parent*

וְשֹׁמֵר תּוֹכַחַת יַעְרִם:

וְשֹׁמֵר    *but one who heeds/guards/keeps*
Qal Ptcp ms שׁמר + conj וְ

תּוֹכַחַת    *reproof/rebuke*

יַעְרִם    *(he) is prudent/shrewd // (he) becomes
prudent/shrewd*
Hiph Impf 3ms ערם

---

Revering YHWH leads to life;
indeed, he'll stay satisfied and will never be touched by harm.

PROV 19:23 ▪ DAY 290

# נַהַם כַּכְּפִיר אֵימַת מֶלֶךְ

| נַהַם | roaring/growling |
|---|---|
| כַּכְּפִיר | like the young lion |
| אֵימַת מֶלֶךְ | terror/dread/fearsomeness of king/ruler |

# מִתְעַבְּרוֹ חוֹטֵא נַפְשׁוֹ׃

| מִתְעַבְּרוֹ | one who angers him |
| | Hith Ptcp ms עבר + conj וְ |
| חוֹטֵא | one who sins/offends/wrongs/endangers |
| | Qal Ptcp ms חטא |
| נַפְשׁוֹ | his life/self/soul |

---

Better a nobody who has a domestic
than one who pretends to be great but lacks comestibles.

PROV 12:9 ▪ DAY 291

מֵשִׁיב דָּבָר בְּטֶרֶם יִשְׁמָע

| | |
|---|---|
| מֵשִׁיב | *one who returns/brings back* |
| | Hiph Ptcp ms שׁוּב |
| דָּבָר | *word/statement/matter* |
| בְּטֶרֶם | *before* |
| יִשְׁמָע | *he hears/listens* |
| | Qal Impf 3ms שׁמע |

אִוֶּלֶת הִיא־לֹו וּכְלִמָּה:

| | |
|---|---|
| אִוֶּלֶת | *folly* |
| הִיא־ | *it/that* |
| לֹו | *to/for him* |
| וּכְלִמָּה | *and disgrace/humiliation* |

---

A dolt spurns his parent's instruction,
but he who heeds reproof becomes prudent.

PROV 15:5 ▪ DAY 292

יֵשׁ בּוֹטֶה כְּמַדְקְרוֹת חָרֶב

| יֵשׁ | there is |
| בּוֹטֶה | one who speaks rashly/thoughtlessly |
| | Qal Ptcp ms בטה |
| כְּמַדְקְרוֹת חָרֶב | like piercings/thrusts of sword |

וּלְשׁוֹן חֲכָמִים מַרְפֵּא׃

| וּלְשׁוֹן חֲכָמִים | but tongue of wise/sage people |
| מַרְפֵּא | gentleness/calmness/healing |

A ruler's redoubtability is like a lion's growling;
he who angers him endangers his life.

PROV 20:2 • DAY 293

## פֹּעַל אוֹצָרוֹת בִּלְשׁוֹן שָׁקֶר

פֹּעַל אוֹצָרוֹת    *acquisition/achievement of*
                  *treasures*

בִּלְשׁוֹן שָׁקֶר    *with/by/through tongue of*
                  *falsehood/deceit/untruth/fraudulence*

## הֶבֶל נִדָּף מְבַקְשֵׁי־מָוֶת׃

הֶבֶל    *breath/vapor/vanity*

נִדָּף    *(that which is) blown away/scattered*
         Niph Ptcp ms נדף

מְבַקְשֵׁי־    *ones who seek*
           Piel Ptcp mp בקש

מָוֶת    *death*

---

He who provides a report before listening—
it shows his stupidity and disgrace.

PROV 18:13 ▪ DAY 294

# שֵׂכֶל אָדָם הֶאֱרִיךְ אַפֹּו

שֵׂכֶל אָדָם     *prudence/wisdom/understanding of*
*man/person*

הֶאֱרִיךְ     *(it) lengthens [i.e., makes slow] //*
*to lengthen [i.e., make slow]*

       Hiph Pf 3ms ארך

       Hiph Inf Cst ארך

אַפֹּו     *his anger*


# וְתִפְאַרְתֹּו עֲבֹר עַל־פָּשַׁע:

וְתִפְאַרְתֹּו     *and his glory/splendor/honor/beauty*

עֲבֹר     *to pass*

       Qal Inf Cst עבר

עַל־פָּשַׁע     *over transgression/offense*

---

There's one who speaks rashly, like sword thrusts;
but the tongue of the enlightened is calm.

PROV 12:18 ▪ DAY 295

אַל־תֶּאֱהַב שֵׁנָה פֶּן־תִּוָּרֵשׁ

| | |
|---|---|
| אַל־תֶּאֱהַב | *do not love* |
| | Qal Impf 2ms אהב |
| שֵׁנָה | *sleep/slumber* |
| פֶּן־ | *lest* |
| תִּוָּרֵשׁ | *you become poor* |
| | Niph Impf 2ms ירשׁ |

פְּקַח עֵינֶיךָ שְׂבַע־לָחֶם:

| | |
|---|---|
| פְּקַח | *open* |
| | Qal Impv ms פקח |
| עֵינֶיךָ | *your eyes* |
| שְׂבַע־ | *be filled/satiated/satisfied* |
| | Qal Impv ms שׂבע |
| לָחֶם | *bread/food* |

# נָחֲלוּ פְתָאיִם אִוֶּלֶת

נָחֲלוּ    *(they) inherit/take possession of/ give as an inheritance*

     נחל Qal Pf 3cp

פְתָאיִם    *simpleminded/naïve/ignorant people*

אִוֶּלֶת    *folly*

# וַעֲרוּמִים יַכְתִּרוּ דָעַת:

וַעֲרוּמִים    *but prudent/shrewd/clever people*

יַכְתִּרוּ    *(they) are crowned*

     כתר Hiph Impf 3mp

דָעַת    *knowledge*

---

A person's prudence makes him wary of getting angry,
and one's glory is to overlook an offense.

PROV 19:11 ▪ DAY 297

תֵּחַת גְּעָרָה בְּמֵבִין

| | |
|---|---|
| תֵּחַת | *(it) goes deep/deeper* |
| | Qal Impf 3fs נחת |
| גְּעָרָה | *rebuke* |
| בְּמֵבִין | *into one who understands/discerns/ perceives* |
| | Hiph Ptcp ms בין + prep בְּ |

מֵהַכּוֹת כְּסִיל מֵאָה:

| | |
|---|---|
| מֵהַכּוֹת | *than to strike* |
| | Hiph Inf Cst נכה + prep מִן |
| כְּסִיל | *fool/dolt/idiot* |
| מֵאָה | *one hundred* |

---

Don't love sleep, lest you become bereft;
open your eyes, be filled with bread.

PROV 20:13 ▪ DAY 298

נָכ֣וֹנוּ לַלֵּצִ֣ים שְׁפָטִ֑ים

| נָכ֣וֹנוּ | *(they) are ready/right/established* |
|---|---|
| | כון Niph Pf 3cp |
| לַלֵּצִ֣ים | *for the scoffers/scorners/mockers* |
| שְׁפָטִ֑ים | *judgments/punishments* |

וּ֝מַהֲלֻמ֗וֹת לְגֵ֣ו כְּסִילִֽים׃

| וּ֝מַהֲלֻמ֗וֹת | *and blows/beatings* |
|---|---|
| לְגֵ֣ו כְּסִילִֽים | *for back of* |
| | *fools/dolts/idiots* |

---

Idiots bestow ignorance as an inheritance,
but the clever are crowned with comprehension.

PROV 14:18 ▪ DAY 299

לְתַאֲוָה יְבַקֵּשׁ נִפְרָד

לְתַאֲוָה *for/after desire/longing/appetite*

יְבַקֵּשׁ *(he) seeks*
Piel Impf 3ms בקשׁ

נִפְרָד *one who is separated/separates himself*
Niph Ptcp ms פרד

בְּכָל־תּוּשִׁיָּה יִתְגַּלָּע:

בְּכָל־תּוּשִׁיָּה *against all sound judgment/success/competence*

יִתְגַּלָּע *he breaks out/bursts out*
Hith Impf 3ms גלע

---

A rebuke descends deeper into a discerning man
than a hundred blows do into a dolt.

PROV 17:10 ▪ DAY 300

# אִישׁ רֵעִים לְהִתְרֹעֵעַ

| אִישׁ | man/person/there are |
|---|---|
| רֵעִים | companions/friends/neighbors |
| לְהִתְרֹעֵעַ | to be friends with/to act as friends/to socialize with |

       לְ prep + (רעה) רעע Hithpoel Inf Cst

    to harm one another/to shatter one another

       לְ prep + רעע Hithpoel Inf Cst

    to shout with joy

       לְ prep + רוע Hithpolel Inf Cst

# וְיֵשׁ אֹהֵב דָּבֵק מֵאָח:

| וְיֵשׁ | and/but there is |
|---|---|
| אֹהֵב | one who likes/loves |

       Qal Ptcp ms אהב

| דָּבֵק | clinging/joined/attached |
|---|---|
| מֵאָח | more than brother/kinsman/relative |

---

Punishments are appointed for scoffers,
and beatings for the backs of boors.

PROV 19:29 ▪ DAY 301

## טֽוֹב אֲרֻחַת יָרָק וְאַהֲבָה־שָׁם

| | |
|---|---|
| טֽוֹב | *better* |
| אֲרֻחַת יָרָק | *ration/allowance/meal of vegetables* |
| וְאַהֲבָה־ | *and love* |
| שָׁם | *there* |

## מִשּׁוֹר אָבוּס וְשִׂנְאָה־בֽוֹ:

| | |
|---|---|
| מִשּׁוֹר | *than ox* |
| אָבוּס | *(one who is) fattened* |
| | Qal Pass Ptcp ms אבס |
| וְשִׂנְאָה־ | *and hatred/enmity* |
| בֽוֹ | *with it* |

---

One who separates himself seeks after a longing;
he fulminates against all sound wisdom.

PROV 18:1 ▪ DAY 302

# אֹרַח חַיִּים לְמַעְלָה לְמַשְׂכִּיל

| | |
|---|---|
| אֹרַח חַיִּים | *way/path of life* |
| לְמַעְלָה | *upward* |
| לְמַשְׂכִּיל | *for one who acts prudently/wisely/with understanding* |

לְ prep + שׂכל Hiph Ptcp ms

# לְמַעַן סוּר מִשְׁאוֹל מָטָּה:

| | |
|---|---|
| לְמַעַן | *in order to* |
| סוּר | *(to) turn away/aside* |

סור Qal Inf Cst

| | |
|---|---|
| מִשְׁאוֹל | *from Sheol/underworld/netherworld* |
| מָטָּה | *below* |

---

There are companions for keeping one company,
but there's a comrade who clings closer than a kinsman.

PROV 18:24 • DAY 303

מַעֲנֶה־רַּךְ יָשִׁיב חֵמָה

| מַעֲנֶה־ | *answer* |
|---|---|
| רַּךְ | *tender/delicate/soft* |
| יָשִׁיב | *(it) turns back* |
| | Hiph Impf 3ms שׁוּב |
| חֵמָה | *wrath/anger/fury* |

וּדְבַר־עֶצֶב יַעֲלֶה־אָף:

| וּדְבַר־עֶצֶב | *but word/statement/speech of hurt/pain* |
|---|---|
| יַעֲלֶה־ | *(it) raises/rises* |
| | Hiph Impf 3ms עלה |
| | Qal Impf 3ms עלה |
| אָף | *anger* |

---

Better a ration of vegetables accompanied by affection
than a fattened ox with enmity.

PROV 15:17 ▪ DAY 304

אַךְ־מְרִי יְבַקֶּשׁ־רָע

| | |
|---|---|
| אַךְ־ | *surely/indeed/only* |
| מְרִי | *rebellion/defiance* |
| יְבַקֶּשׁ־ | *(he) seeks* |
| | בקשׁ Piel Impf 3ms |
| רָע | *evil/bad person* |

וּמַלְאָךְ אַכְזָרִי יְשֻׁלַּח־בּוֹ:

| | |
|---|---|
| וּמַלְאָךְ | *and/but messenger* |
| אַכְזָרִי | *cruel/merciless* |
| יְשֻׁלַּח־ | *(he) will be sent/let loose* |
| | שׁלח Pual Impf 3ms |
| בּוֹ | *against him* |

---

The pathway of life goes upward for one who acts wisely,
turning him away from the underworld below.

PROV 15:24 ▪ DAY 305

## גְּדָל־חֵמָה נֹשֵׂא עֹנֶשׁ

גְּדָל־חֵמָה   *one great of
wrath/anger/fury*

גרל־חֵמָה  KETIV

נֹשֵׂא   *one who bears/pays*

נשׂא Qal Ptcp ms

עֹנֶשׁ   *punishment/fine/penalty*

## כִּי אִם־תַּצִּיל וְעֹוד תֹּוסִף׃

כִּי   *for/because*

אִם־   *if*

תַּצִּיל   *you deliver/rescue*

נצל Hiph Impf 2ms

וְעֹוד   *and again*

תֹּוסִף   *you will add/increase/repeat*

יסף Hiph Impf 2ms

---

A sensitive response reverses wrath,
but noxious speech provokes anger.

PROV 15:1 ▪ DAY 306

גַּם בְּמַעֲלָלָיו יִתְנַכֶּר־נָעַר

| | |
|---|---|
| גַּם | *even/yet/also* |
| בְּמַעֲלָלָיו | *by his acts/deeds* |
| יִתְנַכֶּר־ | *(he) reveals himself/makes himself known/disguises himself* |
| | Hith Impf 3ms נכר |
| נָעַר | *young person/child* |

אִם־זַךְ וְאִם־יָשָׁר פָּעֳלוֹ:

| | |
|---|---|
| אִם־ | *whether* |
| זַךְ | *pure* |
| וְאִם־ | *and whether* |
| יָשָׁר | *upright/right* |
| פָּעֳלוֹ | *his conduct* |

---

A scoundrel surely seeks sedition,
but a merciless messenger will be let loose on him.

PROV 17:11 ▪ DAY 307

מְכַסֶּה־פֶּשַׁע מְבַקֵּשׁ אַהֲבָ֑ה

מְכַסֶּה־     *one who covers*
      Piel Ptcp ms כסה

פֶּשַׁע     *transgression/offense*

מְבַקֵּשׁ     *one who seeks*
      Piel Ptcp ms בקשׁ

אַהֲבָ֑ה     *love*

וְשֹׁנֶה בְדָבָר מַפְרִיד אַלּֽוּף׃

וְשֹׁנֶה     *but one who repeats*
      Qal Ptcp ms שׁנה + conj וְ

בְדָבָר     *matter/word/statement*

מַפְרִיד     *one who separates*
      Hiph Ptcp ms פרד

אַלּֽוּף     *close friend*

---

A bellicose man incurs a penalty;
for if you bail him out, you'll have to do it all over again.

PROV 19:19 ▪ DAY 308

אֱוִלִים יָלִיץ אָשָׁם

| אֱוִלִים | *fools* |
| יָלִיץ | *(he/it) mocks/scorns/scoffs at* |
|  | Hiph Impf 3ms(!) לִיץ |
| אָשָׁם | *guilt/guilt offering* |

וּבֵין יְשָׁרִים רָצוֹן:

| וּבֵין יְשָׁרִים | *but between/among upright people* |
| רָצוֹן | *favor/delight/goodwill* |

---

Even a child reveals himself by his actions,
whether his deportment is decorous and just.

PROV 20:11 • DAY 309

# שִׂנְאָה תְּעוֹרֵר מְדָנִים

| | |
|---|---|
| שִׂנְאָה | *hatred/enmity* |
| תְּעוֹרֵר | *(it) stirs up/awakens/exposes* |
| | Polel Impf 3fs עור |
| מְדָנִים | *contentions* |

# וְעַל כָּל־פְּשָׁעִים תְּכַסֶּה אַהֲבָה:

| | |
|---|---|
| וְעַל כָּל־פְּשָׁעִים | *but over all transgressions/offenses* |
| תְּכַסֶּה | *(it) covers* |
| | Piel Impf 3fs כסה |
| אַהֲבָה | *love* |

One who seeks affection overlooks an offense,
but one who harps on a matter alienates a close friend.

PROV 17:9 ▪ DAY 310

## אֹטֵם אָזְנוֹ מִזַּעֲקַת־דָּל

| | |
|---|---|
| אֹטֵם | *one who closes/stops up* |
| | Qal Ptcp ms אטם |
| אָזְנוֹ | *his ear* |
| מִזַּעֲקַת־דָּל | *from cry/outcry of poor/weak/needy/helpless person* |

## גַּם־הוּא יִקְרָא וְלֹא יֵעָנֶה:

| | |
|---|---|
| גַּם־ | *also/likewise* |
| הוּא | *he/that one* |
| יִקְרָא | *(he) will call out* |
| | Qal Impf 3ms קרא |
| וְלֹא יֵעָנֶה | *but (he) will not be answered* |
| | Niph Impf 3ms ענה |

---

Blockheads scoff at a guilt offering,
but goodwill links the honorable.

PROV 14:9 ▪ DAY 311

## צוּף־דְּבַשׁ אִמְרֵי־נֹעַם

| | |
|---|---|
| צוּף־דְּבַשׁ | *comb of honey* |
| אִמְרֵי־נֹעַם | *words of pleasantness/kindness/favor* |

## מָתוֹק לַנֶּפֶשׁ וּמַרְפֵּא לָעָצֶם:

| | |
|---|---|
| מָתוֹק | *sweet* |
| לַנֶּפֶשׁ | *to the soul/appetite/self* |
| וּמַרְפֵּא | *and gentleness/calmness/healing* |
| לָעָצֶם | *to the bone* |

---

Animus awakens argumentation,
but amity transcends all transgressions.

PROV 10:12 ▪ DAY 312

## לֵץ הַיַּיִן הֹמֶה שֵׁכָר

| | |
|---|---|
| לֵץ | *scoffer/scorner/mocker* |
| הַיַּיִן | *the wine* |
| הֹמֶה | *(one who) is noisy/is tumultuous/ growls/roars/moans* |
| | Qal Ptcp ms המה |
| שֵׁכָר | *strong drink/beer* |

## וְכָל־שֹׁגֶה בּוֹ לֹא יֶחְכָּם:

| | |
|---|---|
| וְכָל־ | *and every* |
| שֹׁגֶה | *one who gets drunk/staggers/goes astray/errs* |
| | Qal Ptcp ms שגה |
| בּוֹ | *with/in it* |
| לֹא יֶחְכָּם | *(he) is not wise/sage* |
| | Qal Impf 3ms חכם |

---

One who plugs his ears against a weak man's wailing—
he too will call out but will not be acknowledged.

PROV 21:13 ▪ DAY 313

# מְשַׁדֶּד־אָב יַבְרִיחַ אֵם

מְשַׁדֶּד־    *one who assaults/acts violently toward/ robs*

     Piel Ptcp ms שׁדד

אָב    *father*

יַבְרִיחַ    *(he) makes flee/drives out*

     Hiph Impf 3ms ברח

אֵם    *mother*

# בֵּן מֵבִישׁ וּמַחְפִּיר:

בֵּן    *son/child*

מֵבִישׁ    *(one) who acts shamefully/causes shame*

     Hiph Ptcp ms בושׁ

וּמַחְפִּיר    *and (one) who acts disgracefully/ shamefully*

     Hiph Ptcp ms חפר + conj וְ

---

Tasteful words are a honeycomb,
sweet to the soul and salubrious to the bones.

PROV 16:24 • DAY 314

רָב־אֹ֫כֶל נִיר רָאשִׁ֑ים

רָב־אֹ֫כֶל *abundance of food*

נִיר רָאשִׁ֑ים *untilled land of poor people/leaders*

Qal Ptcp mp רוש

noun רֹאשׁ

וְיֵ֣שׁ נִסְפֶּ֗ה בְּלֹ֣א מִשְׁפָּֽט׃

וְיֵ֣שׁ *but/and substance/there is*

נִסְפֶּ֗ה *(that which) is swept away/destroyed/ added/increased*

Niph Ptcp ms ספה

בְּלֹ֣א מִשְׁפָּֽט *without justice*

---

Wine's a mocker, liquor roars,
and everyone who staggers from it is out of his wits.

PROV 20:1 ▪ DAY 315

מַתָּן אָדָם יַרְחִיב לֹו

| מַתָּן אָדָם | *gift/present of man/person* |

| יַרְחִיב | *(it) makes room/space* |
| | Hiph Impf 3ms רחב |

| לֹו | *for him* |

וְלִפְנֵי גְדֹלִים יַנְחֶנּוּ:

| וְלִפְנֵי גְדֹלִים | *and before great people* |

| יַנְחֶנּוּ | *it leads/guides him* |
| | Hiph Impf 3ms נחה + 3ms sx |

---

A miscreant and immodest son
mistreats his father and makes his mother move out.

PROV 19:26 ▪ DAY 316

## בָּא־זָדוֹן וַיָּבֹא קָלוֹן

בָּא־    *(it) came*

     Qal Pf 3ms בוא

זָדוֹן    *arrogance/pride*

וַיָּבֹא    *then (it) came*

     Qal wayyiqtol 3ms בוא

קָלוֹן    *shame/dishonor/disgrace*

## וְאֶת־צְנוּעִים חָכְמָה:

וְאֶת־צְנוּעִים    *but with humble/modest people*

חָכְמָה    *wisdom*

Loads of food are latent in the untilled land of the poor,
but substance is swept away by inequity.

PROV 13:23 ▪ DAY 317

עַצְלָה תַּפִּיל תַּרְדֵּמֶה

עַצְלָה    *laziness/sluggishness/sloth*

תַּפִּיל    *(it) makes fall*
     Hiph Impf 3fs נפל

תַּרְדֵּמֶה    *deep sleep/profound slumber*

וְנֶפֶשׁ רְמִיָּה תִרְעָב:

וְנֶפֶשׁ רְמִיָּה    *and soul/person/appetite of*
     *slackness/indolence/negligence/*
     *deceit/treachery*

תִרְעָב    *(it) will be hungry/famished*
     Qal Impf 3fs רעב

---

A man's present makes a place for him,
and it guides him into the presence of the great.

PROV 18:16 ▪ DAY 318

# שְׁמַע עֵצָה וְקַבֵּל מוּסָר

| | |
|---|---|
| שְׁמַע | *hear/listen to/heed* |
| | Qal Impv ms שמע |
| עֵצָה | *counsel/advice* |
| וְקַבֵּל | *and receive/accept* |
| | Piel Impv ms קבל + conj וְ |
| מוּסָר | *instruction/training/education/warning/*<br>*discipline/correction/chastisement* |

# לְמַעַן תֶּחְכַּם בְּאַחֲרִיתֶךָ׃

| | |
|---|---|
| לְמַעַן | *so that* |
| תֶּחְכַּם | *you will be wise/sage* |
| | Qal Impf 2ms חכם |
| בְּאַחֲרִיתֶךָ | *in your end/future* |

---

Conceit came, then came shame;
but insight accompanies the modest.

PROV 11:2 ▪ DAY 319

# אֹגֵר בַּקַּיִץ בֵּן מַשְׂכִּיל

אֹגֵר　　*one who gathers*
　　　　Qal Ptcp ms אגר

בַּקַּיִץ　　*in/during the summer*

בֵּן　　*son/child*

מַשְׂכִּיל　　*(one) who acts prudently/wisely/with understanding*
　　　　Hiph Ptcp ms שׂכל

# נִרְדָּם בַּקָּצִיר בֵּן מֵבִישׁ:

נִרְדָּם　　*one who slumbers profoundly/falls into deep sleep*
　　　　Niph Ptcp ms רדם

בַּקָּצִיר　　*in/during the harvest*

בֵּן　　*son/child*

מֵבִישׁ　　*(one) who acts shamefully/causes shame*
　　　　Hiph Ptcp ms בושׁ

---

Sluggishness plunges one into a deep sleep;
indeed, a slothful soul will starve.

PROV 19:15 ▪ DAY 320

## לֹא־יַחֲרֹךְ רְמִיָּה צֵידוֹ

לֹא־יַחֲרֹךְ    *(he) does not roast*
חרך Qal Impf 3ms

רְמִיָּה    *indolent/negligent person*

צֵידוֹ    *his prey/game/catch*

## וְהוֹן־אָדָם יָקָר חָרוּץ:

וְהוֹן־אָדָם    *but wealth of man/person*

יָקָר    *precious/valuable/honorable*

חָרוּץ    *gold/diligent/industrious/[threshing sledge]*

---

Heed advice and accept instruction
so that you'll become sage over the course of time.

PROV 19:20 • DAY 321

רַע רַע יֹאמַר הַקּוֹנֶה

| | |
|---|---|
| רַע | *bad* |
| רַע | *bad* |
| יֹאמַר | *(he) says*<br>Qal Impf 3ms אמר |
| הַקּוֹנֶה | *the one who buys/acquires*<br>Qal Ptcp ms קנה + article |

וְאֹזֵל לֹו אָז יִתְהַלָּל׃

| | |
|---|---|
| וְאֹזֵל | *but (one who) goes away/going away*<br>Qal Ptcp ms אזל + conj וְ |
| לֹו | *to/for/by himself* |
| אָז | *then* |
| יִתְהַלָּל | *he boasts/praises himself*<br>Hith Impf 3ms הלל |

---

A sagacious son gathers in the summer;
a disgraceful one sleeps deeply during harvest.

PROV 10:5 ▪ DAY 322

לֹעֵג לָרָשׁ חֵרֵף עֹשֵׂהוּ

לֹעֵג     *one who mocks*
Qal Ptcp ms לעג

לָרָשׁ     *the one who is poor*
Qal Ptcp ms רושׁ + article + prep לְ

חֵרֵף     *(he) defies/reviles*
Piel Pf 3ms חרף

עֹשֵׂהוּ     *one who made him*
Qal Ptcp ms עשׂה + 3ms sx

שָׂמֵחַ לְאֵיד לֹא יִנָּקֶה:

שָׂמֵחַ     *one joyful/glad/happy*

לְאֵיד     *at/concerning/about destruction/
disaster/calamity*

לֹא יִנָּקֶה     *(he) will not go unpunished*
Niph Impf 3ms נקה

---

A lazy man won't roast his prey,
but a reputable man's wealth is gold.

PROV 12:27 ▪ DAY 323

# אֹהֵב פֶּשַׁע אֹהֵב מַצָּה

אֹהֵב    *one who loves*
      Qal Ptcp ms אהב

פֶּשַׁע    *transgression/offense*

אֹהֵב    *one who loves*
      Qal Ptcp ms אהב

מַצָּה    *strife*


# מַגְבִּיהַּ פִּתְחוֹ מְבַקֶּשׁ־שָׁבֶר:

מַגְבִּיהַּ    *one who makes high/exalts*
      Hiph Ptcp ms גבה

פִּתְחוֹ    *his opening/door/entrance*

מְבַקֶּשׁ־    *one who seeks*
      Piel Ptcp ms בקשׁ

שָׁבֶר    *destruction/break/crash*

---

"Bad, bad!" says the buyer,
but then he goes on his way and boasts.

PROV 20:14 • DAY 324

זֵד יָהִיר לֵץ שְׁמוֹ

זֵד　　*arrogant/proud person*

יָהִיר　　*haughty/arrogant person*

לֵץ　　*scoffer/scorner/mocker*

שְׁמוֹ　　*his name*


עֹשֶׂה בְּעֶבְרַת זָדוֹן:

עֹשֶׂה　　*one who acts*
　　　　Qal Ptcp ms עשׂה

בְּעֶבְרַת זָדוֹן　　*with/in wrath/rage/anger/fury of*
　　　　　　　　*arrogance/pride*

One who mocks a wretch reviles his maker;
he who delights in disaster won't go unpunished.

PROV 17:5 ▪ DAY 325

נֶ֣זֶם זָ֭הָב בְּאַ֣ף חֲזִ֑יר

| | |
|---:|:---|
| נֶ֣זֶם זָ֭הָב | *ring of gold* |
| בְּאַ֣ף חֲזִ֑יר | *in nose of pig* |

אִשָּׁ֥ה יָ֝פָ֗ה וְסָ֣רַת טָֽעַם׃

| | |
|---:|:---|
| אִשָּׁ֥ה | *woman* |
| יָ֝פָ֗ה | *beautiful* |
| וְסָ֣רַת | *but (one) who turns away/aside* |
| | וְ conj + סור Qal Ptcp fs |
| טָֽעַם | *good sense/taste/discretion* |

---

He who is fond of offense loves strife;
one who elevates his entrance can expect a crash.

PROV 17:19 ▪ DAY 326

## פּוֹטֵר מַיִם רֵאשִׁית מָדוֹן

| | |
|---|---|
| פּוֹטֵר | one who lets out/releases // letting out/releasing |
| | Qal Ptcp ms פטר |
| מַיִם | water |
| רֵאשִׁית מָדוֹן | beginning of strife/contention |

## וְלִפְנֵי הִתְגַּלַּע הָרִיב נְטוֹשׁ׃

| | |
|---|---|
| וְלִפְנֵי | so before |
| הִתְגַּלַּע | breaking out of/bursting out of |
| | Hith Inf Cst גלע |
| הָרִיב | the strife/dispute/quarrel/argument |
| נְטוֹשׁ | desist/quit |
| | Qal Impv ms נטש |

---

A supercilious and snobbish man—"mocker" is his moniker—
he acts in arrogant anger.

PROV 21:24 ▪ DAY 327

יֵשׁ מְפַזֵּר וְנוֹסָף עוֹד

| | |
|---|---|
| יֵשׁ | *there is* |
| מְפַזֵּר | *one who scatters* |
| | Piel Ptcp ms פזר |
| וְנוֹסָף | *and/but one who is added to/increased* |
| | Niph Ptcp ms יסף |
| עוֹד | *again/more* |

וְחוֹשֵׂךְ מִיֹּשֶׁר אַךְ־לְמַחְסוֹר׃

| | |
|---|---|
| וְחוֹשֵׂךְ | *but one who holds back/refrains* |
| | Qal Ptcp ms חשׂךְ + conj וְ |
| מִיֹּשֶׁר | *from uprightness/integrity* |
| אַךְ־ | *surely/indeed/only* |
| לְמַחְסוֹר | *to/for lack/want/deficiency/privation* |

---

A gold ring in a pig's snout:
a pulchritudinous woman who discards discretion.

PROV 11:22 • DAY 328

גַּם מִתְרַפֶּה בִּמְלַאכְתּוֹ

| | |
|---|---|
| גַּם | *also* |
| מִתְרַפֶּה | *one who shows himself slack/lazy/negligent* |
| | Hith Ptcp ms רפה |
| בִּמְלַאכְתּוֹ | *in his work/task* |

אָח הוּא לְבַעַל מַשְׁחִית:

| | |
|---|---|
| אָח | *brother/kinsman/relative/compatriot* |
| הוּא | *he/that one* |
| לְבַעַל מַשְׁחִית | *to master/lord of destruction/ruin* |

---

The commencement of contention is a crack in the dike;
so before a fight flares up, stop.

PROV 17:14 ▪ DAY 329

חַבֻּרוֹת פֶּצַע תַּמְרוּק בְּרָע

| | |
|---|---|
| חַבֻּרוֹת פֶּצַע | *blows/bruises of wound* |
| תַּמְרוּק | *scouring/cleansing* |
| | תמריק KETIV |
| בְּרָע | *for evil* |

וּמַכּוֹת חַדְרֵי־בָטֶן׃

| | |
|---|---|
| וּמַכּוֹת | *and ones that strike* |
| | Hiph Ptcp fp נכה + conj וְ |
| חַדְרֵי־בָטֶן | *rooms/chambers of belly/abdomen/stomach* |

---

There's a man who gives away but gets more,
whereas one who's reluctant to be upright will surely be deficient.

PROV 11:24 ▪ DAY 330

# לְקַח־בִּגְדוֹ כִּי־עָרַב זָר

| | |
|---|---|
| לְקַח־ | *take* |
| | Qal Impv ms לקח |
| בִּגְדוֹ | *his garment* |
| כִּי־ | *for/because/when* |
| עָרַב | *he has become/stood surety for* |
| | Qal Pf 3ms ערב |
| זָר | *stranger* |

# וּבְעַד נָכְרִיָּה חַבְלֵהוּ:

| | |
|---|---|
| וּבְעַד נָכְרִיָּה | *and for/on behalf of foreign/strange/unfamiliar woman* |
| | וּבְעַד נכרים KETIV |
| חַבְלֵהוּ | *take it in pledge/hold him in pledge* |
| | Qal Impv ms חבל + 3ms sx |

---

Likewise, one who's lackadaisical in his duties—
he's a brother to the saboteur.

PROV 18:9 ▪ DAY 331

לִפְנֵי־שֶׁבֶר גָּאוֹן

לִפְנֵי־שֶׁבֶר  *before destruction/break/fracture/crash*

גָּאוֹן  *haughtiness/pride*


וְלִפְנֵי כִשָּׁלוֹן גֹּבַהּ רוּחַ:

וְלִפְנֵי כִשָּׁלוֹן  *and before stumbling/fall/downfall*

גֹּבַהּ רוּחַ  *haughtiness/exaltation of
spirit*

---

Injurious bruises are a scouring for vice,
striking the abdomen's cavities.

PROV 20:30 ▪ DAY 332

יָפִיחַ אֱמוּנָה יַגִּיד צֶדֶק

| | |
|---:|:---|
| יָפִיחַ | *witness of* |
| | noun יָפִיחַ |
| | *he breathes out/pours out* |
| | Hiph Impf 3ms פוח |
| אֱמוּנָה | *honesty/faithfulness* |
| יַגִּיד | *(he) tells* |
| | Hiph Impf 3ms נגד |
| צֶדֶק | *rightness/honesty* |

וְעֵד שְׁקָרִים מִרְמָה:

| | |
|---:|:---|
| וְעֵד שְׁקָרִים | *but witness/testimony of* *falsehoods/deceptions/lies/untruths* |
| מִרְמָה | *deceit/treachery* |

---

Snatch his shirt, for he's stood surety for a stranger,
and on behalf of an unfamiliar woman, take it as security.

PROV 20:16 ▪ DAY 333

חֶ֣סֶד וֶ֭אֱמֶת יִצְּרוּ־מֶ֑לֶךְ

| | |
|---|---|
| חֶ֣סֶד | *lovingkindness/faithfulness/loyalty/ steadfast love/probity* |
| וֶ֭אֱמֶת | *and truth/honesty/trustworthiness/ faithfulness* |
| יִצְּרוּ־ | *(they) guard/protect/preserve* |
| | Qal Impf 3mp נצר |
| מֶ֑לֶךְ | *king/ruler* |

וְסָעַ֖ד בַּחֶ֣סֶד כִּסְאֽוֹ׃

| | |
|---|---|
| וְסָעַ֖ד | *and he maintains* |
| | Qal Pf 3ms סעד + conj וְ |
| בַּחֶ֣סֶד | *by/with/through the loyalty/faithfulness/ lovingkindness/steadfast love/probity* |
| כִּסְאֽוֹ | *his throne* |

---

Vanity eventuates in a crash,
and pomposity of spirit presages a pratfall.

PROV 16:18 ▪ DAY 334

בְּרָב־עָם הֲדַרַת־מֶלֶךְ

| בְּרָב־עָם | in abundance of people/nation |
| הֲדַרַת־מֶלֶךְ | glory/splendor of king/ruler |

וּבְאֶפֶס לְאֹם מְחִתַּת רָזוֹן:

| וּבְאֶפֶס לְאֹם | but in end/lack of people/nation |
| מְחִתַּת רָזוֹן | ruin/terror of prince/[scantness]/[wasting disease] |

An honest deponent declares the truth,
but a weaselly witness, perfidy.

PROV 12:17 ▪ DAY 335

רַק־בְּזָדוֹן יִתֵּן מַצָּה

| | |
|---|---|
| רַק־ | *only/surely* |
| בְּזָדוֹן | *with/through arrogance/pride* |
| יִתֵּן | *(it) gives/produces* |
| | Qal(!) Impf 3ms נתן |
| מַצָּה | *strife* |

וְאֶת־נוֹעָצִים חָכְמָה:

| | |
|---|---|
| וְאֶת־נוֹעָצִים | *but with ones who are counseled/take advice* |
| | Niph Ptcp mp יעץ |
| חָכְמָה | *wisdom* |

---

Fealty and truth protect a potentate,
and it's through troth that he maintains his throne.

PROV 20:28 ▪ DAY 336

## צְדָקָה תְרוֹמֵם־גּוֹי

| | |
|---|---|
| צְדָקָה | *righteousness/truthfulness/justice* |
| תְרוֹמֵם־ | *(it) exalts* |
| | רום Polel Impf 3fs |
| גּוֹי | *nation* |

## וְחֶסֶד לְאֻמִּים חַטָּאת׃

| | |
|---|---|
| וְחֶסֶד לְאֻמִּים | *but disgrace/shame of peoples/nations* |
| חַטָּאת | *sin* |

A ruler's resplendence lies in a robust populace,
but a prince's panic arises from a paucity of people.

PROV 14:28 ▪ DAY 337

מֵשִׁיב רָעָה תַּחַת טוֹבָה

| | |
|---|---|
| מֵשִׁיב | *one who returns* |
| | Hiph Ptcp ms שׁוּב |
| רָעָה | *evil/harm/trouble* |
| תַּחַת טוֹבָה | *for/in place of good* |

לֹא־תָמוּשׁ רָעָה מִבֵּיתוֹ:

| | |
|---|---|
| לֹא־תָמוּשׁ | *(it) will not depart* |
| | Qal Impf 3fs מוּשׁ |
| | KETIV לֹא־תמיש |
| רָעָה | *evil/harm/trouble/calamity/disaster* |
| מִבֵּיתוֹ | *from his house/household/home/ family/dynasty* |

---

Superciliousness surely produces strife,
but sagacity lies with those who take advice.

PROV 13:10 ▪ DAY 338

# עֹשֵׁק־דָּל חֵרֵף עֹשֵׂהוּ

| עֹשֵׁק־ | one who oppresses/exploits/defrauds/ abuses |
| --- | --- |
| | Qal Ptcp ms עשׁק |

| דָּל | poor/weak/needy/helpless person |
| --- | --- |

| חֵרֵף | (he) defies/reviles |
| --- | --- |
| | Piel Pf 3ms חרף |

| עֹשֵׂהוּ | one who made him |
| --- | --- |
| | Qal Ptcp ms עשׂה + 3ms sx |

# וּמְכַבְּדוֹ חֹנֵן אֶבְיוֹן:

| וּמְכַבְּדוֹ | but one who honors him |
| --- | --- |
| | Piel Ptcp ms כבד + 3ms sx + conj וְ |

| חֹנֵן | one who is gracious to/shows mercy to/ takes pity on |
| --- | --- |
| | Qal Ptcp ms חנן |

| אֶבְיוֹן | poor/needy person |
| --- | --- |

---

Integrity dignifies a nation,
but depravity is the disgrace of peoples.

PROV 14:34 ▪ DAY 339

עֵד אֱמוּנִים לֹא יְכַזֵּב

| | |
|---|---|
| עֵד אֱמוּנִים | *witness/testimony of faithfulnesses/honesties* |
| לֹא יְכַזֵּב | *(he/it) does not lie/deceive*<br>Piel Impf 3ms כזב |

וְיָפִיחַ כְּזָבִים עֵד שָׁקֶר׃

| | |
|---|---|
| וְיָפִיחַ | *but witness of*<br>וְ conj + יָפִיחַ noun<br>*but (he/it) breathes out/pours out*<br>Hiph Impf 3ms פוח + conj וְ |
| כְּזָבִים | *lies/falsehoods* |
| עֵד שָׁקֶר | *witness/testimony of falsehood/deceit/untruth/fraudulence* |

---

One who repays help with harm—
harm won't depart from his house.

PROV 17:13 ▪ DAY 340

יַד־חָרוּצִים תִּמְשׁוֹל

יַד־חָרוּצִים    *hand of*
*diligent/industrious people*

תִּמְשׁוֹל    *(it) will rule*
Qal Impf 3fs מָשַׁל

וּרְמִיָּה תִּהְיֶה לָמַס:

וּרְמִיָּה    *but slackness/indolence/negligence/*
*deceit/treachery*

תִּהְיֶה    *(it) will be*
Qal Impf 3fs הָיָה

לָמַס    *for forced labor*

---

He who abuses a beggar mocks his maker,
but one who pities an impoverished person shows him respect.

PROV 14:31 ▪ DAY 341

בְּאֵין אֲלָפִים אֵבוּס בָּר

| | |
|---|---|
| בְּאֵין | *when there are no* |
| אֲלָפִים | *oxen/cattle* |
| אֵבוּס | *trough/manger* |
| בָּר | *clean/grain* |

וְרָב־תְּבוּאוֹת בְּכֹחַ שׁוֹר:

| | |
|---|---|
| וְרָב־תְּבוּאוֹת | *but abundance of yields* |
| בְּכֹחַ שׁוֹר | *in strength/vigor of ox* |

---

Factual testimony doesn't deceive,
but a fraudulent witness exhales lies.

PROV 14:5 ▪ DAY 342

נְהַם כַּכְּפִיר זַעַף מֶלֶךְ

| | |
|---|---|
| נְהַם | *roaring/growling* |
| כַּכְּפִיר | *like the young lion* |
| זַעַף מֶלֶךְ | *rage/vexation of king/ruler* |

וּכְטַל עַל־עֵשֶׂב רְצוֹנוֹ׃

| | |
|---|---|
| וּכְטַל | *but like dew* |
| עַל־עֵשֶׂב | *on grass* |
| רְצוֹנוֹ | *his favor/delight* |

---

The hand of the diligent will govern,
but negligence results in servility.

PROV 12:24 ▪ DAY 343

כַּחֹמֶץ| לַשִּׁנַּיִם וְכֶעָשָׁן לָעֵינָיִם

| כַּחֹמֶץ| | *like the vinegar* |
| לַשִּׁנַּיִם | *to the teeth* |
| וְכֶעָשָׁן | *and like the smoke* |
| לָעֵינָיִם | *to the eyes* |

כֵּן הֶעָצֵל לְשֹׁלְחָיו:

| כֵּן | *so/thus* |
| הֶעָצֵל | *the lazy/sluggish/slothful person* |
| לְשֹׁלְחָיו | *to ones who send him* |

Qal Ptcp mp שלח + 3ms sx + prep לְ

---

A barn is immaculate in the absence of cattle,
but vast yields come from an ox's brawn.

PROV 14:4 ▪ DAY 344

תֻּמַּת יְשָׁרִים תַּנְחֵם

| | |
|---|---|
| תֻּמַּת יְשָׁרִים | *integrity/blamelessness of upright people* |
| תַּנְחֵם | *(it) leads/guides them*<br>Hiph Impf 3fs נחה + 3mp sx |

וְסֶלֶף בּוֹגְדִים יְשָׁדֵּם׃

| | |
|---|---|
| וְסֶלֶף בּוֹגְדִים | *but perversity/twistedness of ones who are treacherous*<br>Qal Ptcp mp בגד |
| יְשָׁדֵּם | *(it) destroys them*<br>Qal Impf 3ms שדד + 3mp sx<br>KETIV ושדם |

---

A ruler's rage is like a lion's roar,
but his favor is like dew upon verdure.

PROV 19:12 ▪ DAY 345

מַתָּן בַּסֵּתֶר יִכְפֶּה־אָף

| | |
|---|---|
| מַתָּן | *gift/present* |
| בַּסֵּתֶר | *in the secrecy/concealed place* |
| יִכְפֶּה־ | *(it) subdues/soothes/averts* |
| | Qal Impf 3ms כפה |
| אָף | *anger* |

וְשֹׁחַד בַּחֵק חֵמָה עַזָּה:

| | |
|---|---|
| וְשֹׁחַד | *and bribe* |
| בַּחֵק | *in the bosom* |
| חֵמָה | *wrath/anger/fury* |
| עַזָּה | *strong* |

---

Like vinegar to the teeth and smoke to the eyes,
so is a slowpoke to those who sent him.

PROV 10:26 ▪ DAY 346

מוֹקֵשׁ אָדָם יָלַע קֹדֶשׁ

| | |
|---|---|
| מוֹקֵשׁ אָדָם | *snare/trap of man/person* |
| יָלַע | *he says rashly* <br> Qal Impf 3ms לעע |
| קֹדֶשׁ | *holiness/holy thing* |

וְאַחַר נְדָרִים לְבַקֵּר:

| | |
|---|---|
| וְאַחַר נְדָרִים | *and after vows* |
| לְבַקֵּר | *to consider* <br> וְ conj + בקר Piel Inf Cst |

---

The guilelessness of the upright guides them,
but the twistedness of the treacherous trounces them.

PROV 11:3 ▪ DAY 347

מֵחֹרֶף עָצֵל לֹא־יַחֲרֹשׁ

מֵחֹרֶף    *from/in winter*

עָצֵל    *lazy/sluggish/slothful person*

לֹא־יַחֲרֹשׁ    *(he) does not plow*
חרשׁ Qal Impf 3ms

וְשָׁאַל בַּקָּצִיר וָאָיִן:

וְשָׁאַל    *and/then he questions/asks*
שׁאל Qal weqatal 3ms
KETIV ישׁאל

בַּקָּצִיר    *in/at the harvest*

וָאָיִן    *and there is nothing*

דִּבְרֵי נִרְגָּן כְּמִתְלַהֲמִים

דִּבְרֵי נִרְגָּן     *words/statements of*
                     *one who gossips/whispers/slanders*

                 Niph Ptcp ms רגן

כְּמִתְלַהֲמִים     *like delicious morsels/delicacies*

                 כְּ + prep להם Hith Ptcp mp


וְהֵם יָרְדוּ חַדְרֵי־בָטֶן:

וְהֵם     *and they*

יָרְדוּ     *(they) descend*

           Qal Pf 3cp ירד

חַדְרֵי־בָטֶן     *rooms/chambers of*
                     *stomach/belly/abdomen*

---

It's a snare to aver brashly, "It's consecrated!"
and to consider it only after vowing.

PROV 20:25 ▪ DAY 349

אָ֣ח נִ֭פְשָׁע מִקִּרְיַת־עֹ֑ז

אָ֣ח　　brother/kinsman/relative

נִ֭פְשָׁע　　(one who is) transgressed against/
offended

　　　　Niph Ptcp ms פשׁע

מִקִּרְיַת־עֹ֑ז　　than city of
strength

וּ֝מִדְיָנִ֗ים כִּבְרִ֥יחַ אַרְמֽוֹן׃

וּ֝מִדְיָנִ֗ים　　and quarrels/contentions

　　　　KETIV ומדונים

כִּבְרִ֥יחַ אַרְמֽוֹן　　like bar of
citadel/fortress

---

An indolent man won't plow in winter;
then, at harvest time, he wonders why there's nothing.

PROV 20:4 ▪ DAY 350

הֹון עָשִׁיר קִרְיַת עֻזֹּו

| הֹון עָשִׁיר | *wealth of rich person* |

| קִרְיַת עֻזֹּו | *city of his strength* |

וּכְחֹומָה נִשְׂגָּבָה בְמַשְׂכִּיתֹו׃

| וּכְחֹומָה | *and like wall* |

| נִשְׂגָּבָה | *(one that is) high* |
| | Niph Ptcp fs שׂגב |

| בְמַשְׂכִּיתֹו | *in his imagination* |

---

A whisperer's words are like delectable delicacies,
and they descend into the abdomen's crevices.

PROV 18:8 ▪ DAY 351

## עֹכֵר בֵּיתוֹ בּוֹצֵעַ בָּצַע

עֹכֵר    *one who troubles*
     Qal Ptcp ms עכר

בֵּיתוֹ    *his house/household/family*

בּוֹצֵעַ    *one who extorts/profits*
     Qal Ptcp ms בצע

בָּצַע    *extortion/profit/unjust gain*

## וְשׂוֹנֵא מַתָּנֹת יִחְיֶה:

וְשׂוֹנֵא    *but one who hates*
     Qal Ptcp ms שׂנא + conj וְ

מַתָּנֹת    *gifts/presents*

יִחְיֶה    *(he) will live*
     Qal Impf 3ms חיה

---

An offended relative is more inaccessible than a strong city,
and quarrels are like a fortress's portcullis.

PROV 18:19 ▪ DAY 352

אֵֽשֶׁת־חֵן תִּתְמֹ֥ךְ כָּבֹ֑וד

| | |
|---|---|
| אֵֽשֶׁת־חֵן | *woman/wife of favor/grace/charm/elegance* |
| תִּתְמֹ֥ךְ | *(she) obtains/gains/takes hold of/holds on to* |
| | תמך Qal Impf 3fs |
| כָּבֹ֑וד | *honor/respect/reputation/glory* |

וְֽעָרִיצִ֗ים יִתְמְכוּ־עֹֽשֶׁר׃

| | |
|---|---|
| וְֽעָרִיצִ֗ים | *and/but ruthless people* |
| יִתְמְכוּ־ | *(they) obtain/gain/take hold of/hold on to* |
| | תמך Qal Impf 3ms |
| עֹֽשֶׁר | *wealth* |

An affluent man's opulence is his mighty city;
it's like a lofty wall in his imagination.

PROV 18:11 ▪ DAY 353

## גָּרֵשׁ לֵץ וְיֵצֵא מָדוֹן

גָּרֵשׁ    *drive out/expel*
גָּרֵשׁ       Piel Impv ms גרשׁ

לֵץ    *scoffer/scorner/mocker*

וְיֵצֵא    *and (it) will go out*
      Qal Impf 3ms יצא + conj וְ

מָדוֹן    *strife/contention*


## וְיִשְׁבֹּת דִּין וְקָלוֹן׃

וְיִשְׁבֹּת    *and (it) will cease*
      Qal Impf 3ms שׁבת + conj וְ

דִּין    *dispute*

וְקָלוֹן    *and shame/dishonor/disgrace*


---

A grafter afflicts his family,
but he who abhors bribes will flourish.

PROV 15:27 ▪ DAY 354

הוֹן מֵהֶבֶל יִמְעָט

הוֹן    *wealth*

מֵהֶבֶל    *than nothingness/vanity/vapor/breath*

יִמְעָט    *(it) will become small/smaller/less*
            Qal Impf 3ms מעט

וְקֹבֵץ עַל־יָד יַרְבֶּה:

וְקֹבֵץ    *but one who gathers*
            Qal Ptcp ms קבץ + conj וְ

עַל־יָד    *on/upon/by/beside hand/portion*

יַרְבֶּה    *(he) makes much/increases*
            Hiph Impf 3ms רבה

---

A graceful dame obtains distinction,
but the ruthless seize riches.

PROV 11:16 ▪ DAY 355

תַּחֲנוּנִים יְדַבֶּר־רָשׁ

| תַּחֲנוּנִים | *supplications* |
|---|---|

יְדַבֶּר־　*(he) speaks*
　　　　　Piel Impf 3ms דבר

רָשׁ　*one who is poor*
　　　Qal Ptcp ms רוש

וְעָשִׁיר יַעֲנֶה עַזּוֹת:

וְעָשִׁיר　*but rich person*

יַעֲנֶה　*(he) answers/speaks up*
　　　Qal Impf 3ms ענה

עַזּוֹת　*strong things/harshly*

---

Expel a scoffer, and rivalry will leave,
and dispute and disgrace will cease.

PROV 22:10 ▪ DAY 356

מְקַלֵּל אָבִיו וְאִמּוֹ

| | |
|---|---|
| מְקַלֵּל | *one who curses* |
| | Piel Ptcp ms קלל |
| אָבִיו | *his father* |
| וְאִמּוֹ | *and his mother* |

יִדְעַךְ נֵרוֹ בֶּאֱשׁוּן חֹשֶׁךְ׃

| | |
|---|---|
| יִדְעַךְ | *(it) will go out/be extinguished* |
| | Qal Impf 3ms דעך |
| נֵרוֹ | *his lamp* |
| בֶּאֱשׁוּן חֹשֶׁךְ | *in/at time/pupil of darkness* |
| | KETIV בְּאִישׁוּן חֹשֶׁךְ |

---

Money dissipates faster than the mist,
but one who sets it aside can make much.

PROV 13:11 ▪ DAY 357

# זוֹרֵעַ עַוְלָה יִקְצָר־אָ֑וֶן

| | |
|---|---|
| זוֹרֵעַ | *one who sows* |
| | Qal Ptcp ms זרע |
| עַוְלָה | *injustice/dishonesty/iniquity* |
| יִקְצָר־ | *(he) will reap/harvest* |
| | Qal Impf 3ms קצר |
| | KETIV  יקצור־ |
| אָ֑וֶן | *iniquity/injustice/sin/evil/trouble/ misfortune/harm* |

# וְשֵׁבֶט עֶבְרָתוֹ יִכְלֶה:

| | |
|---|---|
| וְשֵׁבֶט עֶבְרָתוֹ | *and rod of his wrath/rage/anger/fury* |
| יִכְלֶה | *(it) will come to an end/fail* |
| | Qal Impf 3ms כלה |

---

An impecunious man utters supplications,
but a rich man replies with impudence.

PROV 18:23 ▪ DAY 358

מִדְיָנִים יַשְׁבִּית הַגּוֹרָל

| מִדְיָנִים | *quarrels/contentions* |
|---|---|

| יַשְׁבִּית | *(it) makes cease* |
|---|---|

Hiph Impf 3ms שבת

| הַגּוֹרָל | *the lot* |
|---|---|

וּבֵין עֲצוּמִים יַפְרִיד:

| וּבֵין עֲצוּמִים | *and between/among strong/mighty people* |
|---|---|

| יַפְרִיד | *it separates* |
|---|---|

Hiph Impf 3ms פרד

---

He who damns his dad and mom—
his lamp will go out in pitch-dark gloom.

PROV 20:20 ▪ DAY 359

אָמַ֣ר עָצֵל אֲרִ֣י בַח֑וּץ

| | |
|---|---|
| אָמַ֣ר | *(he) says* |
| | Qal Pf 3ms אמר |
| עָצֵל | *lazy/sluggish/slothful person* |
| אֲרִ֣י | *lion* |
| בַח֑וּץ | *outside/in the street* |

בְּת֥וֹךְ רְ֝חֹב֗וֹת אֵרָצֵֽחַ׃

| | |
|---|---|
| בְּת֥וֹךְ רְ֝חֹב֗וֹת | *in midst/middle of streets/squares* |
| אֵרָצֵֽחַ | *I will be slain/killed* |
| | Niph Impf 1cs רצח |

---

He who sows inequity will reap iniquity,
and the rod of his fury will fail.

PROV 22:8 ▪ DAY 360

מֹנֵעַ בָּר יִקְּבֻהוּ לְאֹום

| מֹנֵעַ | one who withholds |
|---|---|

Qal Ptcp ms מנע

| בָּר | grain |
|---|---|

| יִקְּבֻהוּ | (they) will curse him |
|---|---|

Qal Impf 3mp קבב + 3ms sx

| לְאֹום | people/nation |
|---|---|

וּבְרָכָה לְרֹאשׁ מַשְׁבִּיר:

| וּבְרָכָה | but blessing |
|---|---|

| לְרֹאשׁ מַשְׁבִּיר | for head of<br>one who sells grain |
|---|---|

Hiph Ptcp ms שבר

---

The lot puts an end to litigiousness,
and it splits up strong men.

PROV 18:18 ▪ DAY 361

## נַחֲלָה מְבֹהֶלֶת בָּרִאשֹׁנָה

נַחֲלָה     *inheritance/property*

מְבֹהֶלֶת     *(that which is) hastily obtained*
Pual Ptcp fs בהל

בָּרִאשֹׁנָה     *in/at the beginning*

## וְאַחֲרִיתָהּ לֹא תְבֹרָךְ׃

וְאַחֲרִיתָהּ     *and/then its end/future*

לֹא תְבֹרָךְ     *(it) will not be blessed*
Pual Impf 3fs ברך

---

An indolent man says, "There's a lion outside!
I'll be slain in the streets!"

PROV 22:13 • DAY 362

# תִּפְאֶרֶת בַּחוּרִים כֹּחָם

| | |
|---|---|
| תִּפְאֶרֶת בַּחוּרִים | *glory/splendor/honor/beauty of young people* |
| כֹּחָם | *their strength/vigor* |

# וַהֲדַר זְקֵנִים שֵׂיבָה:

| | |
|---|---|
| וַהֲדַר זְקֵנִים | *and glory/splendor/honor/majesty of old people* |
| שֵׂיבָה | *old age/gray hair* |

---

A nation curses him who withholds grain,
but a blessing is for the head of him who sells it.

PROV 11:26 ▪ DAY 363

Property procured in haste at first—
its future won't be blessed.

PROV 20:21 • DAY 364

The splendor of the young is their strength,
and the honor of the aged is their silver hair.

PROV 20:29 • DAY 365

# ALPHABETICAL INDEX OF HEBREW WORDS

# FREQUENCY INDEX OF HEBREW WORDS

## WORDS OCCURRING ON 52 DAYS

יהוה  4, 20, 21, 30, 37, 45, 47, 53, 66, 67, 68, 71, 72, 77, 84, 85, 90, 99, 107, 114, 116, 154, 155, 158, 159, 161, 162, 163, 164, 165, 167, 174, 183, 188, 195, 200, 202, 204, 207, 213, 214, 216, 217, 223, 234, 236, 237, 238, 263, 269, 276, 290

רָשָׁע  4, 15, 16, 17, 29, 30, 31, 35, 41, 44, 60, 71, 73, 81, 82, 86, 93, 95, 96, 97, 152, 153, 154, 155, 156, 157, 163, 168, 170, 172, 173, 175, 176, 179, 180, 181, 183, 185, 186, 187, 189, 190, 205, 206, 208, 209, 215, 219, 221, 231, 243, 250

## WORD OCCURRING ON 49 DAYS

צַדִּיק  15, 16, 17, 29, 31, 39, 41, 43, 44, 46, 49, 52, 55, 73, 81, 82, 86, 88, 96, 110, 152, 154, 155, 156, 157, 163, 166, 168, 170, 172, 173, 175, 176, 179, 180, 181, 185, 187, 190, 191, 200, 201, 205, 206, 209, 211, 240, 253, 265

## WORD OCCURRING ON 48 DAYS

לֵב  1, 9, 19, 28, 31, 32, 38, 40, 42, 67, 68, 70, 74, 78, 79, 80, 83, 89, 98, 109, 152, 158, 159, 160, 161, 162, 165, 166, 169, 171, 174, 177, 178, 182, 186, 192, 194, 198, 199, 202, 222, 227, 235, 245, 251, 258, 268, 286

## WORD OCCURRING ON 40 DAYS

אִישׁ  5, 10, 12, 33, 34, 40, 51, 62, 66, 67, 69, 72, 74, 75, 76, 83, 87, 92, 100, 101, 102, 113, 127, 153, 160, 164, 169, 178, 193, 199, 220, 224, 230, 232, 233, 242, 247, 260, 264, 281

## WORD OCCURRING ON 38 DAYS

טוֹב  1, 5, 16, 18, 25, 29, 33, 37, 46, 61, 69, 72, 75, 76, 78, 84, 88, 103, 115, 156, 160, 167, 169, 171, 191, 192, 195, 212, 239, 246, 249, 262, 277, 278, 280, 288, 291, 304

## WORD OCCURRING ON 31 DAYS

שָׂפָה  11, 12, 18, 32, 34, 38, 43, 70, 77, 79, 80, 91, 94, 105, 106, 111, 117, 129, 157, 166, 177, 196, 203, 228, 242, 244, 252, 267, 270, 272, 273

## WORD OCCURRING ON 30 DAYS

פֶּה  11, 12, 15, 22, 28, 33, 36, 69, 70, 73, 76, 91, 95, 152, 157, 178, 189, 193, 196, 201, 203, 208, 210, 211, 223, 226, 230, 244, 256, 266

## WORDS OCCURRING ON 29 DAYS

דֶּרֶךְ  2, 4, 6, 10, 59, 66, 68, 75, 93, 123, 126, 153, 159, 160, 162, 164, 170, 184, 188, 210, 213, 214, 224, 239, 241, 257, 274, 283, 289

כְּסִיל   2, 7, 9, 11, 18, 23, 28, 32, 34, 36,
50, 56, 89, 91, 92, 98, 136, 182,
197, 218, 225, 228, 233, 248,
259, 271, 282, 300, 301

## WORDS OCCURRING ON 27 DAYS

חָכָם   6, 19, 23, 32, 36, 39, 42, 50, 54,
56, 58, 70, 79, 94, 100, 118, 121,
141, 177, 196, 219, 225, 226,
248, 254, 261, 295

נֶפֶשׁ   1, 7, 11, 13, 22, 33, 35, 39, 59, 64,
101, 155, 175, 179, 184, 194, 203,
212, 222, 229, 247, 257, 266,
287, 293, 314, 320

## WORD OCCURRING ON 26 DAYS

כֹּל   24, 30, 49, 66, 87, 90, 104, 106,
108, 120, 134, 161, 165, 167, 168,
171, 197, 207, 216, 217, 232, 255,
275, 302, 312, 315

## WORD OCCURRING ON 25 DAYS

רַע   7, 17, 35, 43, 99, 108, 125, 156,
167, 168, 171, 176, 184, 204,
225, 227, 231, 238, 240, 246,
279, 290, 307, 324, 332

## WORD OCCURRING ON 19 DAYS

דַּעַת   9, 19, 20, 28, 32, 34, 36, 58, 112,
119, 135, 197, 201, 212, 220, 226,
267, 285, 299

## WORDS OCCURRING ON 18 DAYS

אָדָם   5, 9, 51, 69, 110, 158, 159, 162,
174, 188, 198, 207, 248, 274,
297, 318, 323, 349

חַיִּים   8, 15, 26, 27, 39, 63, 81, 121, 128,
133, 235, 237, 241, 258, 261, 284,
290, 305

## WORDS OCCURRING ON 17 DAYS

גַּם   3, 30, 46, 85, 94, 107, 154, 164,
210, 212, 243, 251, 256, 287,
309, 313, 331

כִּי   48, 57, 97, 98, 103, 104, 158,
172, 210, 221, 229, 252, 266,
271, 279, 308, 333

עשׂה   21, 48, 52, 57, 77, 85, 90, 92,
102, 132, 140, 197, 215, 221, 325,
327, 341

## WORDS OCCURRING ON 16 DAYS

אֱוֶלֶת   2, 9, 23, 26, 28, 36, 74, 102, 122,
159, 197, 233, 245, 254, 294,
299

דָּבָר   20, 37, 76, 106, 111, 131, 144,
169, 173, 189, 193, 275, 294,
306, 310, 351

יָשָׁר   6, 10, 71, 82, 105, 138, 153, 184,
189, 208, 224, 250, 283, 309,
311, 347

עַיִן   6, 20, 35, 66, 85, 103, 108, 117,
167, 186, 192, 218, 255, 272, 298,
346

## WORDS OCCURRING ON 15 DAYS

בֵּן   50, 54, 55, 88, 119, 124, 130, 143,
158, 229, 234, 259, 282, 316, 322

פָּנֶה   10, 28, 29, 45, 83, 87, 109, 153,
156, 198, 218, 284, 318, 329, 334

## WORDS OCCURRING ON 14 DAYS

אהב   1, 3, 4, 27, 38, 105, 113, 118, 120,
124, 285, 298, 303, 326

אַף   97, 102, 104, 115, 122, 158, 172,
252, 260, 271, 297, 306, 328,
348

בִין   2, 19, 28, 80, 89, 94, 112, 135,
153, 177, 188, 218, 275, 300

חָכְמָה   2, 45, 53, 80, 89, 92, 112, 182,
193, 211, 218, 262, 319, 338

מֶלֶךְ 14, 38, 57, 100, 105, 108, 161, 219, 244, 284, 293, 336, 337, 345

צְדָקָה 4, 8, 21, 57, 61, 63, 93, 123, 126, 138, 139, 215, 241, 339

רֵעַ 3, 35, 38, 40, 75, 87, 120, 137, 150, 170, 198, 201, 253, 303

## WORDS OCCURRING ON 13 DAYS

אֱוִיל 6, 26, 42, 65, 79, 94, 117, 166, 196, 226, 232, 292, 311

מוּסָר 26, 45, 54, 119, 124, 125, 128, 142, 194, 245, 285, 292, 321

רָצוֹן 14, 68, 71, 72, 77, 84, 105, 157, 236, 249, 284, 311, 345

## WORDS OCCURRING ON 12 DAYS

בַּיִת 17, 42, 47, 181, 185, 250, 254, 276, 278, 288, 340, 354

יָד 27, 48, 69, 132, 161, 165, 182, 240, 254, 256, 343, 357

לָשׁוֹן 22, 27, 31, 36, 78, 133, 174, 211, 270, 273, 295, 296

מִשְׁפָּט 21, 29, 41, 52, 60, 61, 95, 216, 217, 221, 244, 317

רֹאשׁ 3, 5, 18, 24, 62, 90, 101, 104, 132, 317, 325, 358

שֵׂכֶל 14, 17, 37, 47, 58, 70, 111, 130, 255, 274, 305, 322

שֶׁקֶר 77, 147, 173, 215, 228, 230, 252, 270, 273, 296, 335, 342

תּוֹעֵבָה 4, 7, 57, 68, 71, 77, 97, 99, 107, 154, 165, 236

## WORDS OCCURRING ON 11 DAYS

הָלַךְ 18, 34, 55, 56, 74, 75, 118, 129, 131, 213, 289

רוּחַ 42, 66, 109, 115, 122, 131, 133, 220, 277, 281, 334

רָעָה 30, 63, 78, 149, 152, 187, 191, 242, 249, 272, 340

שָׁמַע 6, 54, 85, 101, 119, 121, 163, 194, 264, 294, 321

## WORDS OCCURRING ON 10 DAYS

אָב 47, 50, 54, 136, 143, 163, 259, 292, 316, 359

אַיִן 24, 53, 64, 112, 146, 182, 185, 190, 344, 350

רַב 3, 24, 25, 67, 87, 122, 137, 166, 181, 195

שָׁמַר 1, 22, 59, 128, 142, 184, 196, 203, 257, 292

## WORDS OCCURRING ON 9 DAYS

אִשָּׁה 47, 84, 151, 254, 259, 278, 280, 328, 355

בּוֹא 86, 91, 97, 180, 235, 243, 249, 253, 319

בקש 19, 28, 112, 249, 296, 302, 307, 310, 326

הוּא 18, 103, 144, 153, 228, 265, 287, 313, 331

כּוּן 57, 110, 140, 153, 162, 263, 269, 270, 301

לֵץ 54, 58, 112, 118, 135, 301, 315, 327, 356

מָוֶת 10, 27, 63, 100, 139, 187, 241, 261, 296

שֵׂנֵא 3, 102, 104, 124, 125, 173, 279, 285, 354

תְּבוּנָה 1, 40, 53, 74, 92, 98, 122, 199, 220

## WORDS OCCURRING ON 8 DAYS

אֵת 56, 164, 191, 216, 218, 277, 319, 338

חֶסֶד 5, 8, 51, 204, 246, 247, 336, 339

**WORDS OCCURRING ON 3 DAYS**

**WORDS OCCURRING ON 4 DAYS**

| | | | | | | | |
|--:|:--|--:|:--|--:|:--|--:|:--|
| 270 | עַד | 353 | מַשְׂכִּית | 200 | מִגְדָּל | 259 | טרד |
| 178 | עוה | 331 | מַשְׁחִית | 180 | מְגוֹרָה | 294 | טֶרֶם |
| 360 | עוֹלָה | 235 | משׁך | 280 | מִדְבָּר | 327 | יָהִיר |
| 204 | עָוֹן | 171 | מִשְׁתֶּה | 312 | מִדְיָן | 190 | יְסוֹד |
| 312 | עוּר | 314 | מָתוֹק | 295 | מַדְקֵרָה | 229 | יסר |
| 153 | עֹז | 354 | מַתָּנָה | 195 | מְהוּמָה | 139 | יעל |
| 265 | עָלָה | 177 | מָתַק | 340 | מוֹשׁ | 328 | יָפֶה |
| 205 | עָלַץ | 292 | נאץ | 182 | מְחִיר | 267 | יָקָר |
| 185 | עָמַד | 335 | נגד | 281 | מַחֲלֶה | 220 | יְקָר |
| 266 | עָמָל | 296 | נדף | 234 | מַחְסֶה | 225 | ירא |
| 266 | עָמֵל | 349 | נֵדֶר | 305 | מַטֶּה | 287 | ירה |
| 308 | עֹנֶשׁ | 211 | נוב | 332 | מַכָּה | 304 | יָרָק |
| 272 | עצה | 248 | נָוֶה | 288 | מָלֵא | 298 | ירשׁ |
| 361 | עָצוּם | 328 | נֶזֶם | 331 | מְלָאכָה | 238 | ישׁע |
| 320 | עֲצֻלָה | 193 | נַחַל | 284 | מַלְקוֹשׁ | 252 | יֶתֶר |
| 237 | עָקֵב | 300 | נחת | 282 | מֵמֶר | 251 | כְּאָב |
| 289 | עקשׁ | 329 | נטשׁ | 363 | מנע | 281 | כול |
| 230 | עֶרֶב | 309 | נכר | 343 | מַס | 202 | כוּר |
| 198 | עֲרֻבָּה | 333 | נָכְרִי | 184 | מְסִלָּה | 342 | כזב |
| 355 | עָרִיץ | 276 | נסח | 214 | מָעוֹז | 217 | כִּיס |
| 345 | עֵשֶׂב | 276 | נצב | 357 | מעט | 267 | כְּלִי |
| 346 | עָשָׁן | 264 | נֵצַח | 244 | מַעַל | 294 | כְּלִמָּה |
| 330 | פזר | 207 | נְשָׁמָה | 305 | מַעַל | 348 | כפה |
| 257 | פַּח | 241 | נְתִיבָה | 309 | מַעֲלָל | 242 | כרה |
| 329 | פטר | 160 | סוג | 174 | מַעֲרָךְ | 211 | כרת |
| 161 | פֶּלֶג | 269 | סוּס | 176 | מָצוֹד | 334 | כִּשָּׁלוֹן |
| 217 | פֶּלֶס | 190 | סוּפָה | 188 | מִצְעָד | 299 | כתר |
| 298 | פֶּן | 283 | סלל | 202 | מַצְרֵף | 351 | להם |
| 255 | פנה | 336 | סעד | 167 | מָקוֹם | 213 | לוז |
| 278 | פִּנָּה | 317 | ספה | 222 | מֹרָה | 325 | לעג |
| 267 | פְּנִינִים | 149 | סתר | 307 | מְרִי | 349 | לעע |
| 332 | פֶּצַע | 348 | סֵתֶר | 104 | מֵרַע | 300 | מֵאָה |
| 290 | פקד | 284 | עָב | 332 | מרק | 192 | מָאוֹר |
| 298 | פקח | 268 | עבד | 283 | מְשֻׂכָה | 194 | מאס |

# Index of Verses from the Book of Proverbs

| | | | | | |
|---|---|---|---|---|---|
| 13:5 | DAY 173 | 14:17 | DAY 102 | 15:21 | DAY 74 |
| 13:6 | DAY 123 | 14:18 | DAY 299 | 15:23 | DAY 76 |
| 13:7 | DAY 24 | 14:19 | DAY 156 | 15:24 | DAY 305 |
| 13:8 | DAY 101 | 14:20 | DAY 3 | 15:25 | DAY 276 |
| 13:9 | DAY 96 | 14:21 | DAY 150 | 15:26 | DAY 99 |
| 13:10 | DAY 338 | 14:22 | DAY 246 | 15:27 | DAY 354 |
| 13:11 | DAY 357 | 14:23 | DAY 106 | 15:28 | DAY 152 |
| 13:12 | DAY 235 | 14:24 | DAY 23 | 15:29 | DAY 163 |
| 13:13 | DAY 144 | 14:25 | DAY 13 | 15:30 | DAY 192 |
| 13:14 | DAY 261 | 14:26 | DAY 234 | 15:31 | DAY 121 |
| 13:15 | DAY 239 | 14:28 | DAY 337 | 15:32 | DAY 194 |
| 13:16 | DAY 197 | 14:29 | DAY 122 | 15:33 | DAY 45 |
| 13:17 | DAY 231 | 14:30 | DAY 258 | 16:1 | DAY 174 |
| 13:18 | DAY 142 | 14:31 | DAY 341 | 16:2 | DAY 66 |
| 13:19 | DAY 7 | 14:32 | DAY 187 | 16:3 | DAY 263 |
| 13:20 | DAY 56 | 14:33 | DAY 89 | 16:4 | DAY 30 |
| 13:21 | DAY 191 | 14:34 | DAY 339 | 16:5 | DAY 165 |
| 13:22 | DAY 88 | 14:35 | DAY 14 | 16:6 | DAY 204 |
| 13:23 | DAY 317 | 15:1 | DAY 306 | 16:7 | DAY 164 |
| 13:24 | DAY 124 | 15:2 | DAY 36 | 16:8 | DAY 61 |
| 13:25 | DAY 179 | 15:3 | DAY 167 | 16:9 | DAY 162 |
| 14:1 | DAY 254 | 15:4 | DAY 133 | 16:10 | DAY 244 |
| 14:2 | DAY 213 | 15:5 | DAY 292 | 16:11 | DAY 217 |
| 14:3 | DAY 196 | 15:6 | DAY 181 | 16:12 | DAY 57 |
| 14:4 | DAY 344 | 15:7 | DAY 32 | 16:13 | DAY 105 |
| 14:5 | DAY 342 | 15:8 | DAY 71 | 16:14 | DAY 100 |
| 14:6 | DAY 112 | 15:9 | DAY 4 | 16:15 | DAY 284 |
| 14:7 | DAY 34 | 15:10 | DAY 125 | 16:16 | DAY 262 |
| 14:8 | DAY 2 | 15:11 | DAY 158 | 16:17 | DAY 184 |
| 14:9 | DAY 311 | 15:12 | DAY 118 | 16:18 | DAY 334 |
| 14:10 | DAY 222 | 15:13 | DAY 109 | 16:19 | DAY 277 |
| 14:11 | DAY 250 | 15:14 | DAY 28 | 16:20 | DAY 37 |
| 14:12 | DAY 10 | 15:15 | DAY 171 | 16:21 | DAY 177 |
| 14:13 | DAY 251 | 15:16 | DAY 195 | 16:22 | DAY 26 |
| 14:14 | DAY 160 | 15:17 | DAY 304 | 16:23 | DAY 70 |
| 14:15 | DAY 275 | 15:18 | DAY 260 | 16:24 | DAY 314 |
| 14:16 | DAY 225 | 15:19 | DAY 283 | 16:26 | DAY 266 |